PRE-WAR 1619–1819

Seeds of War Sown Early!

I have been u[illegible] Africa. After a horribl[illegible] hold of a ship, here I am o[illegible] land, at the hands of a white-skinned and cruel people. They say I am their slave, that they can buy and sell me at will. Surely no good can come from such an idea.—**Ella**, August 1619, Jamestown, VA

I is the Infant, from the arms
Of its fond mother torn,
And at a public auction sold
With horses, cows, and corn.

Z is a Zealous man, sincere,
Faithful, and just, and true;
An earnest pleader for the slave—
Will you not be so too?

We declare slavery illegal.
—Rhode Island, 1652

Slaves are hereby declared "real estate."
—State of Virginia, 1705

I have frequently seen [slaves] whipt to that degree that large pieces of their skin have been hanging down their backs, yet I never observed one of them to shed a tear.—**John Brickell**

For months and months at a time we weren't allowed off the farm. Sometimes we would get as far as the gate and peep over. We were told that if we got outside the Padirollers would get us.—**Uriah Bennett**, slave

I haven't anything to say against slavery. My old folks put my clothes on me…they gave me shoes and stockings and put them on me when I was a little boy. I loved them, and I can't go against them in anything. There were things I did not like about slavery on some plantations, whuppin' and sellin' parents and children from each other, but I haven't much to say. I was treated good.
—**Samuel Riddick**

Slaves bring the judgment of Heaven on a country.—**George Mason**

I's just follow the finger. The white man point his finger and I follow it and do.—**Cuffee**, slave

In 1776 Thomas Jefferson signed the Declaration of Independence, which states "all men are created equal." Jefferson was a slave owner.

SOLD!

I didn't come to America to get along with other people from all over and from other states. What do I care about them? I came for opportunity for me and my family. I'm all for fast progress, and bigger cities, and more work. What do I have in common with those hick farmers in the South—nothing. To the Devil with them!—**blacksmith**, Rhode Island

I was an early victim of slave trading. I was born in Benin, in what is now Nigeria, in 1745. At age 11, I was kidnapped from my family and sold into slavery. Later I was sold again to traders and chained on a slave ship bound for America. I was sold to a Virginia planter, and then to a British naval officer, and finally to a Philadelphia merchant who gave me the chance to buy my freedom. As a ship's steward, I traveled widely. I also worked to bring an end to the slave trade. In 1791, I wrote my autobiography.—**Gustavus Vassa**

Laws, I gots to be up at dawn's crack with the baby to head to the fields. That sun sho is hot. Massa says we gots to pick fast today. Cotton is back-breakin' work. It's just one row after another. Gots to stop to nurse the baby as I can, but so the 'seer can't see me.—**Lizzie**, 17, plantation slave

Eli Whitney invents the cotton gin, 1793.

Eli Whitney's invention of the cotton gin made it possible for farmers to make more money and harvest more cotton each year. But it also meant farmers needed more workers. So, they bought slaves from Africa to tend their fields. The cotton gin revolutionized farming…and slavery.

The Fugitive Slave Act of 1793 demands the return of runaway slaves.

1820–1860 Antebellum="Before the War"

I don't know why some people can't understand the unity of the South. We have our own identity and traditions. Cotton is my crop and I need my slaves to make a successful living. If those darn Yankees came down here they'd see it's a lot of hot, hard hand-labor, no machine to magically get our crop in and meet the worldwide demand for cotton. Cotton is King, after all!—**plantation owner**, South Carolina

abolitionist: person who worked to do away with slavery

Slavery is a covenant with death and an agreement with hell.—abolitionist **William Lloyd Garrison**, *The Liberator,* Boston

COTTON IS KING!

Some people say "The South was built on the backs of blacks."

It's like this: they's good massas and bad massas. Most white folks not slaves, but be about as po' as we slaves are! My plantation family's good to me.—**slave cook**, Louisiana

Antislavery newspapers began in 1821 with white editor Benjamin Lundy's *Genius of Universal Emancipation*. It had six subscribers.

Slavery was sometimes called a "necessary evil" or the "peculiar institution."

Reveille is a bugle call that was used to wake up sleeping soldiers at sunrise. During the Civil War, the call was sounded between 4:45-6:00 in the morning! When the last note played, the flag was raised, a gunshot was fired, and the soldiers had to be dressed and ready for roll call.

I can't believe a man like that can be President of these United States! Andrew Jackson is nothing but a common man. Newspapers call him a "barbarian," "half-wit," and "tyrant," and I must say, I agree with them. The people got what they wanted, I guess…a low-class man running this whole nation!—**U.S. citizen**, 1828

A plot that involved 9,000 blacks, led by free black Denmark Vesey, was exposed in Charleston, South Carolina in 1822. Vesey and 36 others were executed.

Only one of every 20 Northerners was an active abolitionist.

I didn't have to be told that if a slave struck his master it meant death. Freeborn in North Carolina, but the son of a slave father, I knew slavery firsthand. My hatred of slavery drove me to Boston, where I sold old clothes and subscriptions to the *Freedom's Journal*. I burned to deliver my own message and in 1829 published my pamphlet, *Walker's Appeal*.—**David Walker**

In 1831, slave Nat Turner led 70 blacks in a revolt that slaughtered 57 men, women, and children in rural Southampton County, Virginia. Troops rushed in to put down the uprising and killed over one hundred blacks—the innocent as well as the insurrectionists—in a savage massacre. Wild rumors and alarms swept through the South—could this happen again?!—**newspaperman**, North Carolina

I didn't know I was a slave until I found out I couldn't do the things I wanted.—Edmund, Georgia

…Virginia declares slaves are "property"…New York puts runaway slaves to death…1725 …Virginia grants slaves right to form own church…1739…Slave

black woman to lecture against slavery…William Lloyd Garrison publishes the first edition of the newspaper, Liberator, which called for emancipation of slaves…Nat Turner leads a slave rebellion in Southampton, Virginia…1833…The American and

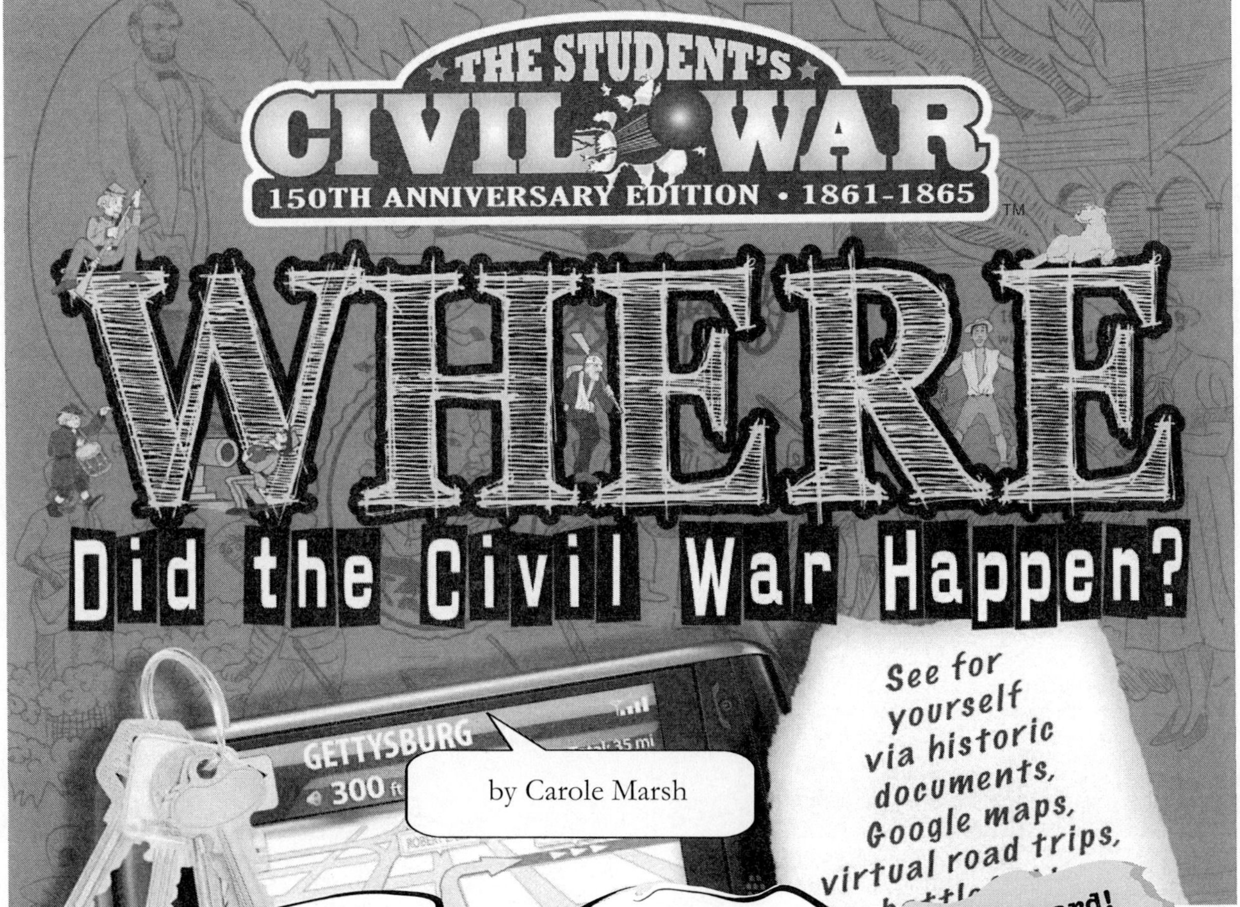

Southerners were polite in calling slavery a "necessary evil." I call slavery a "positive good." I stand by what I said in Congress—slavery is good for blacks!—**John C. Calhoun**, South Carolina senator, 1837

Boo! Boo!

I was born a slave. I worked long and hard for my master 22 years. I finally ran away, and been hiding in a small space in my grandmother's attic for seven years. I'm trying to get to the North and gain my freedom. I finally have my chance. A boat is going to take me there tonight. Perhaps by morning, I'll be free!—**Harriet Jacobs**, North Carolina

How Come?

When I was born I was black.
When I grew up I was black.
When I'm sick I'm black.
When I go out into the sun I'm black.
When I die I'll be black.

But you:
When you were born you were pink.
When you grow up you are white.
When you get sick you are green.
When you go out in the sun you are red.
When you go out in the cold you are blue.
When you die you turn purple.
And you call me colored?

$50 Reward!

Ranaway from the Subscriber, living in the county of Edgecombe, NC, about eight miles north of Tarborough, on the 24th of August last, a negro fellow named Washington, about 24 years of age, 5 feet and 8 or 10 inches high, dark complexion, stout built, and an excellent field hand, no particular marks about him recollected.

Maybe he's on the railroad?

sesquicentennial: (noun) [ses-kwi-sen-ten-ee-uhl] a 150th anniversary or its celebration

Runaways Held in the New Bern, NC, Jail

Two New Negro Men, the one named Joe, about 45 years of age...much wrinkled in the face, and speaks bad English. The other is a young fellow...speaks better English than Joe, whom he says is his father, has a large scar on the fleshy part of his left arm.... They have nothing with them but an old Negro cloth jacket and an old blue sailor's jacket without sleeves. Also...a Negro named Jack, about 23 years of age...of a thin visage, blear-eyed...has six rings of his country marks around his neck, his ears are full of holes.

I was born on a plantation near Fayetteville, North Carolina, and I belonged to J.B. Smith. He owned about 30 slaves. When a slave was no good, he was put on the auction block in Fayetteville and sold.
—**Sarah Louise Augustus**

What man can make, man can unmake.—**Frederick Douglass**, abolitionist

rebellion in South Carolina; 44 slaves killed...1777...Vermont outlaws slavery...1783...Massachusetts outlaws slavery...1792...Kentucky joins Union as slave

the Female Anti-Slavery Societies are formed in Philadelphia...1833...Oberlin College is the first coed college founded to educate African Americans...1837...The first Anti-Slavery Convention of American Women is held in New

I thought it was the Year of the Tiger.
No, that was last year.
Oh.

It takes an army to do a book. Here's ours:

HEADQUARTERS
Gen. Michele Yother, Gen. Mike Longmeyer, Master Sergeant Cowboy Pilot Bob Longmeyer
Indispensible Right Hand (Wo)man: Nancy "You Gotta Have" Hart

All you really need is heart, you know.
I know.

CIVIL WAR CENTRAL
Chief Wrangler: Paige Muh
Sergeant at Art Arms: John Hanson
Scribes, First Class: Whitney Akin, Janice Baker, Sherri Smith Brown
(Battle) Field Artists: Vicki DeJoy, Corie Ferguson, Yvonne Ford, Randolyn Friedlander, Jessica Talley
Erstwhile Intern: Emily Kimbell

John's relative walked home from the Civil War.
Oh, I thought he drove a Volkswagon.

That's the important people, right?
Absolutely.

GENERAL & ACCOUNTING
Muster Masters: Marcie Comeau, Cindy Green, Bri Roden

War bonds, right?
Sure, wanna buy some?
Yeah, my old Confederate currency ok?

SALES
Melessa Hill, Pam Morris, Gina Vranesevich, Lori White, Valerie Curry, Jennifer Johnson
Hallelujah Chorus: Denise Morris

MARKETING MILITIA
Head of the One-Million-Man E-mail March: Camille Chasteen
Linda Metoyer, Mark Dean, Tammy Weeks, Jennifer Kelly, Justin Badger

PRODUCTION & FULFILLMENT
Colonel James Barnard
Dave Guerrero, Pernell Arnold, Kathy Morgan, Jeff Jerabeck

I need fulfilling.
You always do.

SPECIAL UNIT
Hair and Makeup: Christina Yother
Dance and Funny Faces: Grant Yother
Cheerleader: Avery Longmeyer
PT, Boot Camp, and Gymastics: Ella Longmeyer
Best Boy: Evan "Da? Da?!" Longmeyer

I could use a makeover.
Ya think?
My kinda guy!
Cute legs!
Whata sweetheart!
I thought he was the key grip.
That, too.

Private First Class: CAROLE MARSH

Shouldn't she go up at the top?
It's safer down here...out of the line of fire.
I'm just sayin...

In 1849, there were 15 Northern and 15 Southern states. There were more people in the North, but since each state had 2 senators, there was a "stalemate" in the Senate at that time for any effort to pass laws.

I remember all the bricklayers; they all was colored... The men that plastered the City Hall outside and put those columns up in the front...they was slaves, mos' all the fine work...was done by slaves. They called 'em artisans. None of 'em could read, but give 'em any plan an' they could foller it to the las' line.—**John H. Jackson**

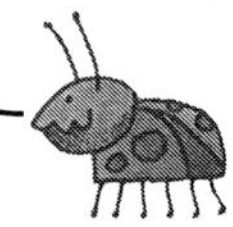

Carole Marsh Civil War and Other Sassy Books for Young Readers are available from your favorite school supply or teacher store, almost all of America's fine museum and park stores, at lovely bookstores everywhere, or if all else fails, direct from www.gallopade.com, or call 1-800-536-2GET (that's 2438), extension 11, Miss Cindy.

For further information, trade terms, rights sales, good recipes, advice, and more, please contact:
GALLOPADE INTERNATIONAL
6000 Shakerag Hill
Suite 314
Peachtree City, Georgia
30269

You mean like when the wife stood on the hill and waved her hankie welcoming her Johnny home from the war?
The very same!
That's in the South, right?
Yes.
They made up that town name, right?
Probably.

See our bibliography and more at www.studentscivilwar.com

I had to try to put an end to this political battle! When the territory of California applied to join the Union in 1849—as a free state—the U.S. had half free and half slave states. To stop this madness, I introduced a bill that would let California be a free state. However, my Compromise of 1850 also said that any new state could choose to be free or slave based on "popular sovereignty" or what the people wanted. After all, a state should have the right to decide what it wants to be, right? My bill passed, but alas, it was only a temporary solution.—Senator **Henry Clay**, Kentucky

state...1793...The Fugitive Slave Act forces return of runaway slaves...Eli Whitney invents the cotton gin...1796...Tennessee joins Union as slave state...1800

York...1839...Joseph Cinque leads a successful revolt on the slave ship, Amistad...1850...Congress passes the Fugitive Slave Act requiring captured runaway slaves to be returned to their owners. Whites now hunt slaves for profit...

A Word from the Author

There's a song that goes *"War! What's it all about? Absolutely nothing!"*

However war is usually about *something*. As you know, the Revolutionary War was all about America wrenching herself away from the final grasp of her mother country of England. It was a war to secure freedom, a new nation, and a new way of life. Later, no one looked back and said, "Hey, maybe we shouldn't have fought that war."

Close to a hundred years after America's founding, people were restless. America was now about a lot of ways of life, many quite different from the others. You might be a plantation owner using slave labor to grow your cotton crop. You might be a mountain woman still living in the wilds of Appalachia. You could be a president trying to run the still new, young, ambitious, and sometimes, even cantankerous and disagreeable country.

Two of the major disagreements of the mid-1800s were slavery and states' rights versus federal rights. Some folks said that they could not survive without slave labor, that they were good to their slaves, and that slavery was now a necessary and permanent part of American life. Others said slavery was wrong and that there was no reason any human being should be owned by another. After all, wasn't America about freedom for all people?

Some Americans thought that states should be able to make their own decisions without so much interference from the federal government in Washington. (Sound familiar?) Other Americans insisted that's what Washington and the federal government were for: to keep all states fair and equal and to solve disputes.

You could say that lanky, teenage America had major growing pains! But America was no longer a "kid." America was at a serious crossroads. Would Americans fight their fellow Americans over these issues? Could such disagreements be resolved by talking, cooperation, compromise, and change? Or would we go to war?

What a curious turn of events—to believe you had to fight your fellow countrymen to the death! Wasn't there any other way? As we know today, getting along and solving problems is much better than going to war. Sometimes, if you are under attack, you may feel you have no choice but to go to war to defend your nation, or to defend others.

Let's just say it was complicated. By the spring of 1861, Americans were actually talking about going to war. They made it sound necessary, even exciting. Many believed it would be a quick war—with their side winning, naturally!

Of course, it didn't happen that way. It was a long war—four years—with terrible tragedies. Slavery was ended. But not before most people "took sides" and fought face-to-face, often against people they knew or were related to, until no one any longer felt that war was a good thing, not even a so-called "necessary" war.

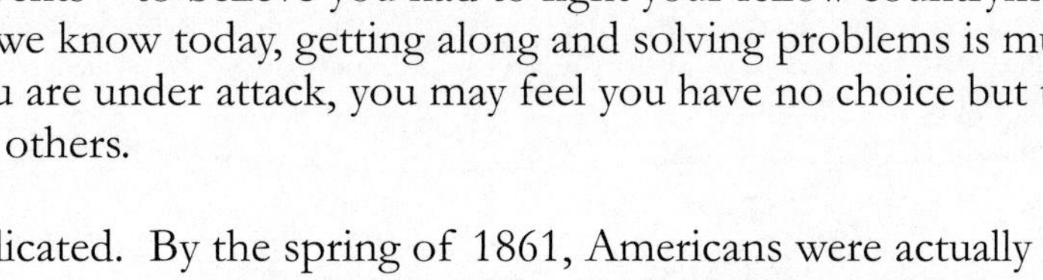

What eventually led to war was a long, drawn out, complex, contradictory set of circumstances, actions, misunderstandings, and oversights. Could we have ended slavery and preserved the union—without war? Think about this, for it may be your job to assess, decide, act or not act, or argue for or against some similar situation one day!

As you read, imagine being that person at that time, in that place during that event. How would you feel, what would you do, how would you change? Today, could we possibly still "stumble" into such a long war? Would around-the-clock news make a difference? Would gathering those who disagree around a table and negotiating work? Diplomacy? The Civil War contains a world of wondering!

What was the American Civil War about? What did it mean? Was there another way? Was it fun, exciting? Was it fair? Who won? Who lost? What would you have done? What do you think?

Why does it matter what *you* think? Because in the absence of diplomacy, cooperation, collaboration, compromise, understanding, honor, and integrity, it is war, not peace, that always looms on our horizon. The past was in their hands. The future is in yours.

Carole Marsh
Shakerag Hill
Peachtree City, Georgia

Reader,

After you read this book, you can go online to www.studentscivilwar.com and learn more.

Ask your school or public librarian to help you find resources for your age!

I've heard rumors of war going around lately. People whispering about soldiers, weapons, strategies. Some even say I've sparked their interest. They want to fight the South and end all the slavery right now. It's the book, I guess. When I wrote Uncle Tom's Cabin, I didn't expect it to be so controversial. I just knew the story needed to be told. I wanted people to know what life was really like for slaves, with good owners and bad owners from Southern and Northern towns. I think I really got people thinking. Most have never heard slavery described like this before.—**Harriet Beecher Stowe**

I am **Tom**, a fictional character from Ms. Stowe's famous book about how slaves were mistreated. In her story, I was murdered in cold blood by plantation overseer Simon Legree. Did such things happen in real life? Were they common or rare? What do you think?

I'm **Franklin Pierce**, elected president in 1852, but not strong enough to lead our nation through the gathering storm of war!

Nine months I was trying to get away.—**Solomon Northup**, slave, born free in New York, kidnapped in 1841 and enslaved on a cotton plantation near Red River in Louisiana.

I find it so hard to believe that Americans might fight Americans! North or South, we are all countrymen, neighbors, brothers, sisters, friends—how can war be? And yet I feel this volcanic groundswell growing beneath the very soil of the land. Will all these eternal arguments over slavery, state versus federal rights, and more just grow louder until we are not talking, but fighting?—**new mother**, Georgia

This footer is a Civil War timeline on top and an African American timeline on the bottom.

Territory, fueling debate over slave status...1808...Congress outlaws slave trade; slavery persists...1812...Louisiana joins Union as slave state...1816... Indiana

her first book of verse...1857...With the Dred Scott Decision, the U.S. Supreme Court denies citizenship to black people...1859...White abolitionist, John Brown, leads a raid at Harper's Ferry. He is captured and sentenced to death...1861...Civil

WHAT

Did the United States Look Like in 1861?

Before the Civil War began in April 1861, the United States was already a divided nation. Some states in the Union allowed slavery, some did not. Once the war began, eleven of the slave states left the Union. Four slave states (known as border states) remained in the Union.

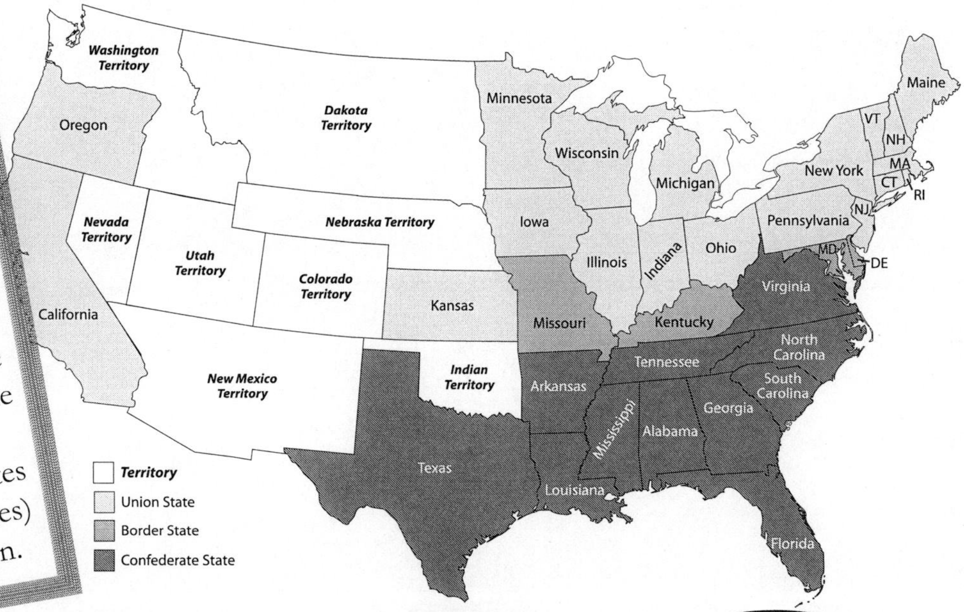

UNITED WE STAND! DIVIDED WE FALL

The math doesn't add up, does it—13 stars on the Confederate flag and only 11 states in the Confederacy?

I'll tell you what happened—Missouri and Kentucky didn't secede from the Union, but secessionists within each state sent representatives to our Confederate Congress! —
South Carolina merchant

In 1861, most of the U.S. population was concentrated east of the Mississippi River. Notice all those wide-open spaces out West!

	Total IN UNION	Total OUT OF UNION
Dec 1860; SC secedes	32	-1
Jan 1861; MS, FL, AL, GA, LA secede	27	-6
Jan 1861; KS admitted to Union	28	
Feb 1861; TX secedes	27	-7
Apr 1861; WAR!		
Apr-Jun 1861; VA, AR, NC, TN secede	23	-11

joins Union as free state...1817...Mississippi joins Union as slave state...1818...Illinois joins Union as free state...1819...Alabama joins Union as slave state...

War begins...Charlotte Forten Grimke becomes a volunteer teacher of freed men on St. Helena Island in South Carolina...1863...Harriet Tubman leads a military raid on the Combahee River in South Carolina and helps hundreds of slaves escape

WHERE Was the Mason Dixon Line?

The Mason-Dixon line is located at approximately 39° 43' 20" mean latitude and runs east-west.

You've heard of it; now where exactly is it? The Mason-Dixon line is usually thought of as the line that divides the North and the South. Before the Civil War, the southern boundary of Pennsylvania was considered the dividing line between slave states and free states. The Mason-Dixon line actually is the boundary line that separates Pennsylvania from Maryland and part of West Virginia, and the boundary between Maryland and Delaware. Confused? Let's look!

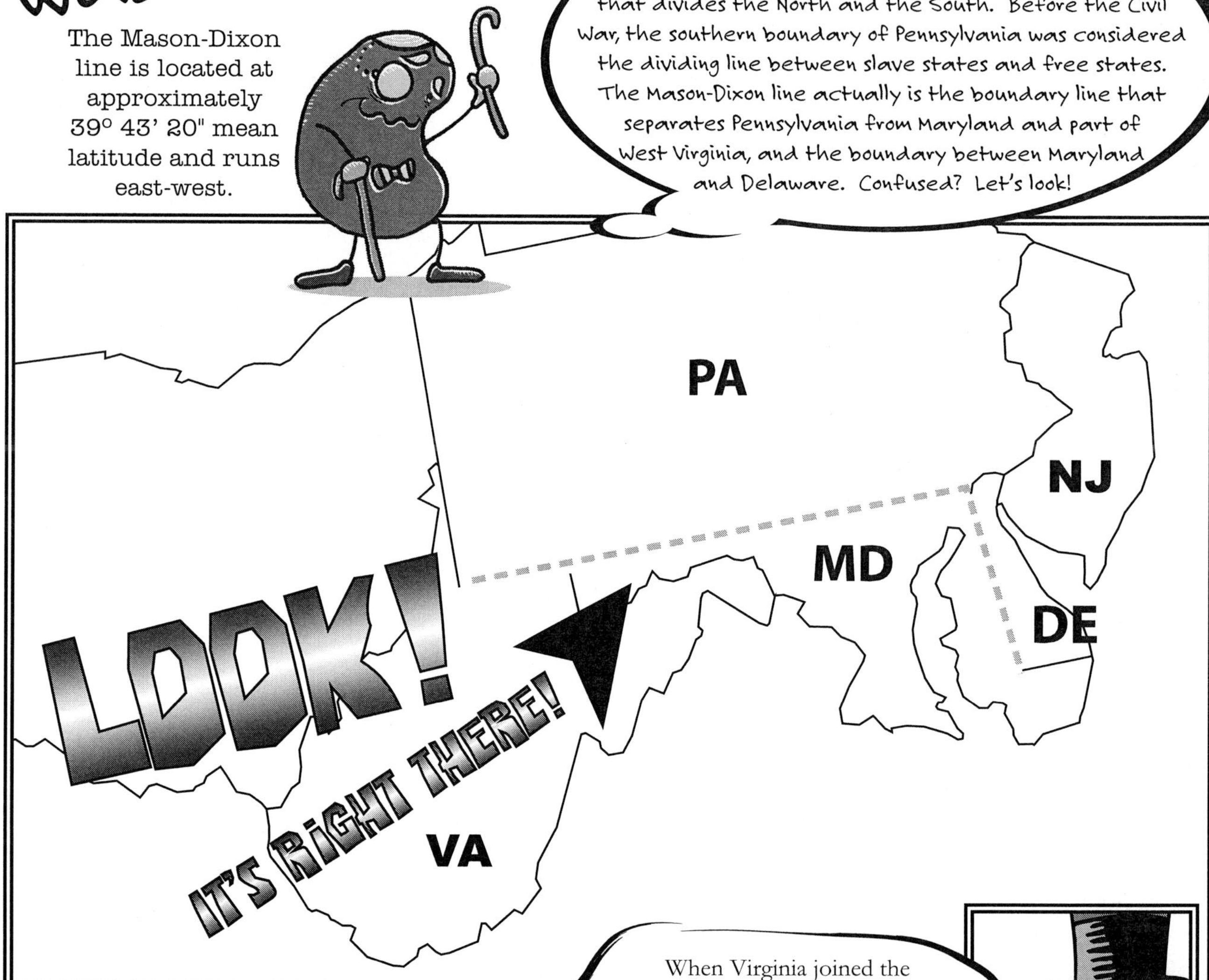

In 1861, about 22 million people lived in the North, and about 9 million lived in the South (and about 3.5 million of those were slaves!).

Advantage: North!

When Virginia joined the Confederacy, I was very concerned about what Maryland would do. Why, if Maryland left the Union, Washington, D.C. would be surrounded by Confederate territory! So I called for Union forces to come and defend the nation's capital. Fortunately, Maryland remained in the Union.

—President Abraham Lincoln

1820...The Missouri Compromise admits Maine to Union as free state, Missouri as slave state, and prohibits slavery north of Missouri...1821... Missouri

to freedom...1865...The Thirteenth Amendment abolishes slavery...The Freedmen's Bureau is established by Congress...1872...The Freedmen's Bureau is abolished by Congress...1877...The Hayes Compromise ends Reconstruction by

Where Were the CAPITALS?

The capital of the Confederacy was moved from Montgomery, Alabama to Richmond, Virginia very early in the war. Confederate leaders felt that their capital should be closer to the upper Southern states, where the heaviest fighting would most likely take place.

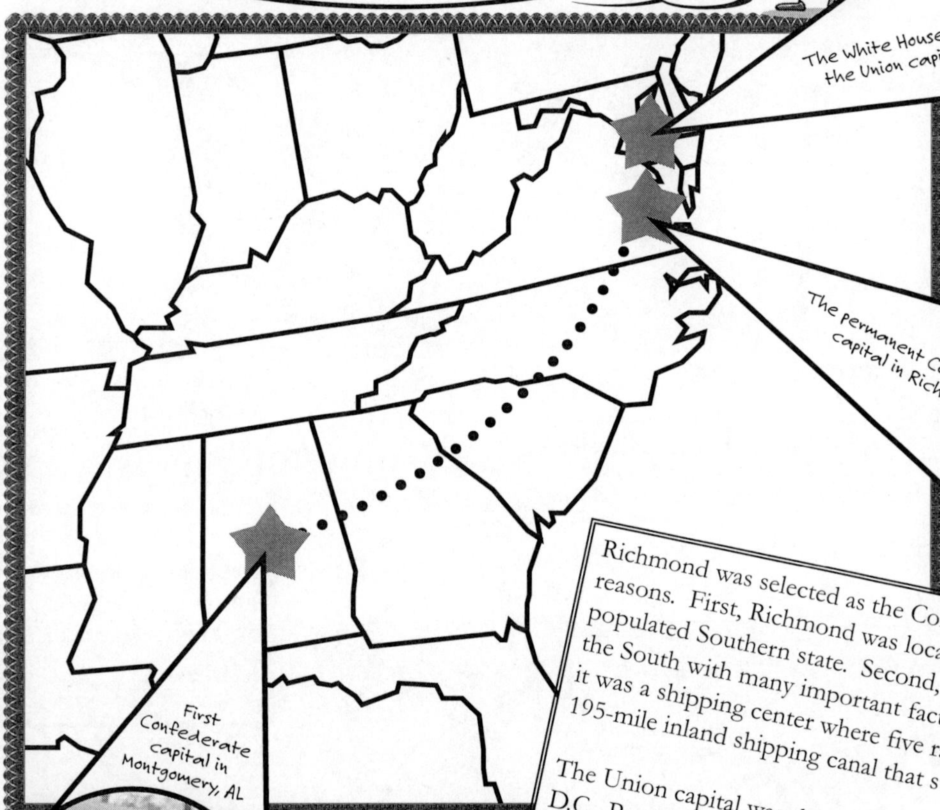

Oh boy! They didn't have to go far to fight each other!

Richmond was selected as the Confederate capital for several other reasons. First, Richmond was located in the richest and most highly populated Southern state. Second, it was the manufacturing center of the South with many important factories and machine shops. Third, it was a shipping center where five railroads converged, and had a 195-mile inland shipping canal that stretched west into the mountains.

The Union capital was the capital of the United States—Washington, D.C. President Abraham Lincoln, commander-in-chief, oversaw the war from the White House.

After Richmond was captured, President Lincoln walked around the first floor of the White House of the Confederacy for about three hours. He did not go to the second floor, feeling it was improper to visit the private quarters of Jefferson Davis' home.

Our president, Jefferson Davis, and his wife Varina, live right here in Richmond, in the White House of the Confederacy! Two of his children have been born here, too! We're right proud of this house.
—Richmond schoolmistress

A capital idea!

Where Was the FIRST BATTLE of the Civil War?

Fort Sumter, South Carolina was the site of the first shot fired in the Civil War on April 12, 1861! The fort stood on an island in the harbor of Charleston, South Carolina. This meant that it was a FEDERAL fort standing in CONFEDERATE territory!

Fort Sumter had been a symbol for both the North and the South since December 1860, when South Carolina became the first Southern state to secede from the Union.

The crisis reached its peak when President Lincoln ordered that supplies be sent to the fort. Confederates chose to fire on the fort rather than allow it to be resupplied.

Fort Sumter was one of a series of forts built after the War of 1812 to protect the southern U.S. coastline. Its five brick sides were five feet thick. The fort was able to house 650 men and support more than 130 guns!

I'd never seen anything like that in my life! Bombs exploding, fires blazing—what a sight! We climbed to rooftops and balconies to watch the spectacle. And, of course, we were so pleased when the South was victorious!

—Charleston resident

Fort Sumter was named after Thomas Sumter, an officer in the Revolutionary War. He was known as "the Gamecock of the Revolution"!

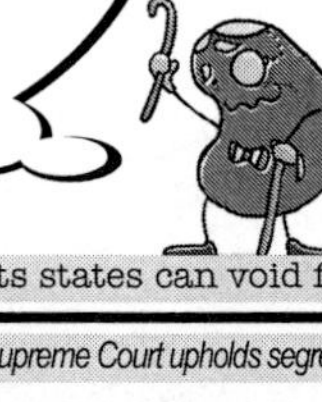

outlaws slavery...1828...South Carolina insists states can void federal laws...1830...Congress debates states' rights vs. federal government...1831...Abolitionist

Conference of Colored Women is held in Boston...1896...The U.S. Supreme Court upholds segregation in its "separate but equal" doctrine set forth in the Plessy vs. Ferguson case...Mary Church Terrell graduates from the Women's Medical

The Geography of WAR

Jagged mountains, deep valleys, raging rivers, dense forests—geography has always played a major role in the outcome of war. Controlling high ground, waterways, or a mountain pass provide a major advantage to any army. During the Civil War, before airplanes, helicopters, and satellite photos, geography was a key factor in the strategy of the Union army.

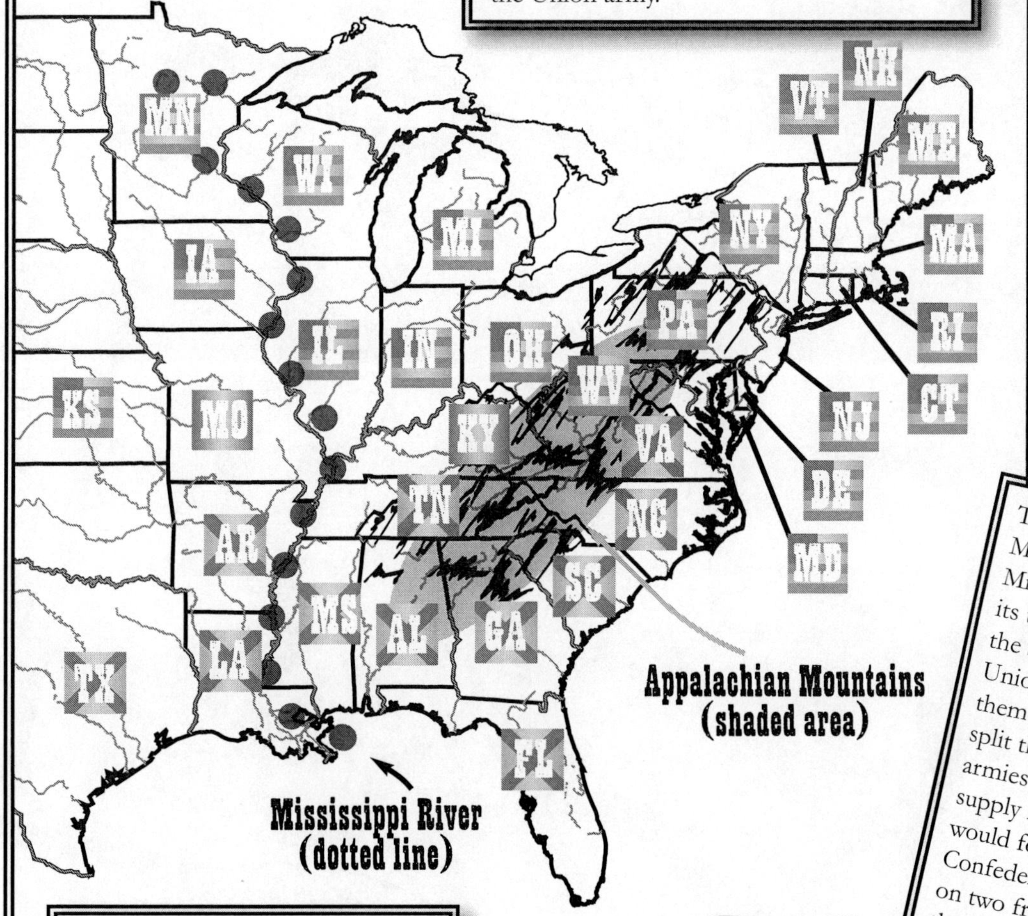

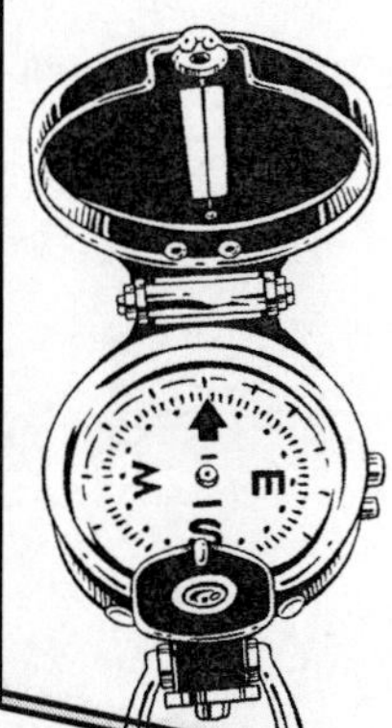

The Appalachian Mountains and Mississippi River (and its tributaries) divided the South. If the Union could control them both, they could split the Southern armies and close off supply routes. This would force the Confederates to fight on two fronts, divide their manpower, and make them vulnerable.

Most battles were fought on Confederate land. The Union army's goal was to invade the South and defeat the Confederacy. Its strategy?

Divide and conquer!

Because we were so aware of geography, we named many battles after nearby landmarks. The Rebs didn't. For example, we named the Battle of Bull Run for a nearby creek, while the Rebs called it the Battle of Manassas for a nearby town. Makes no sense to me!
—Union major

Where Was the UNION BLOCKADE?

The Confederate states had a very long coastline—about 3,500 miles along the Atlantic Ocean and the Gulf of Mexico! The Union navy set up a blockade along the Southern coast to keep supplies from arriving by ship. The blockade also attempted to stop Confederate merchant ships from traveling to Europe to sell important products like cotton.

blockade: use of military forces to close ports

In the 1700s Blackbeard blockaded the port of Charleston, South Carolina! The "Fiercest Pirate of Them All?"

—The very same!

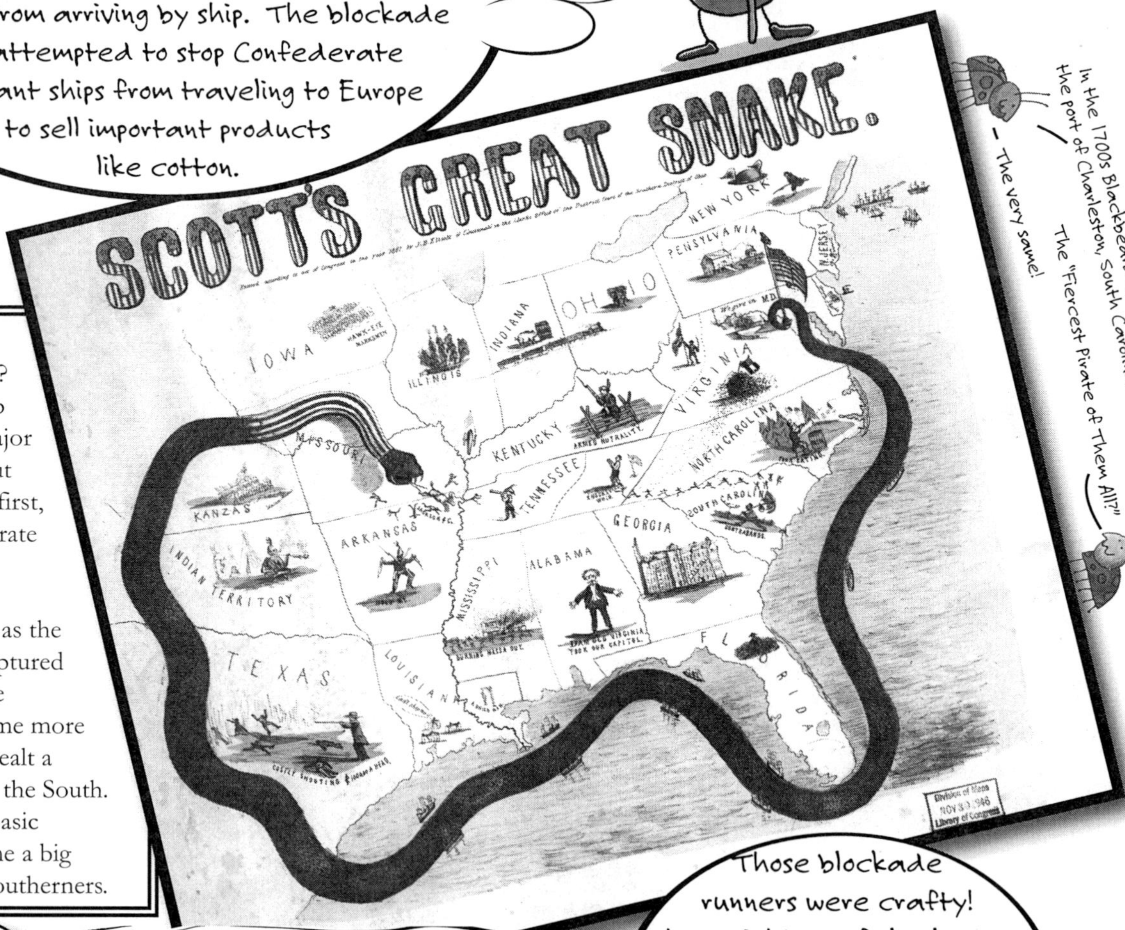

Did the blockade work? It was a big job to guard 10 major ports and about 200 inlets. At first, many Confederate ships slipped through the blockade. But as the Union navy captured more ships, the blockade became more effective and dealt a severe blow to the South. Shortages of basic supplies became a big problem for Southerners.

Those blockade runners were crafty! They might use false lantern signals, change the nameplates on their ships, or even fly flags from other countries to fool the Union navy patrols!

What a way to make big money! I've got a fast ship, a crafty crew, and we sneak in and out of Southern ports at night delivering the supplies they are dying for—like rifles, medicine, blankets, shoes, you name it! Frankly, my dear, it's a blast!
—Rhett Butler, Southern blockade runner (fictional character in *Gone With the Wind*)

Southern-made shoes were not made very well, so Southerners welcomed good-quality imported shoes—especially those with left and right feet!

Northern industry...South Carolina nullifies federal edict, calls for secession...President Jackson declares no states may leave Union...1833...Lucretia Mott

Southern states to gather life histories of ex-slaves...1940...Ella Jo Baker, a dedicated organizer in the freedom movement, begins work in the South as field secretary of the NAACP...1941...Civil Rights Movement begins...Thousands of black

Where Did SOLDIERS Come From?

What is the most important resource in fighting a war? Manpower! The population of the North was much higher than the South, so there were simply more men available to fight. The Union army numbered about 2,100,000. The Confederates had about 800,000-900,000 soldiers.

Even though the North held a three-to-one advantage in manpower, the South had a secret weapon—good military training. At that time, most of the leading military schools were located in the South: Virginia Military Institute (VMI) in Lexington; The Citadel in Charleston, South Carolina; and the Louisiana Military Academy at Baton Rouge. Many graduates of those schools were career military officers.

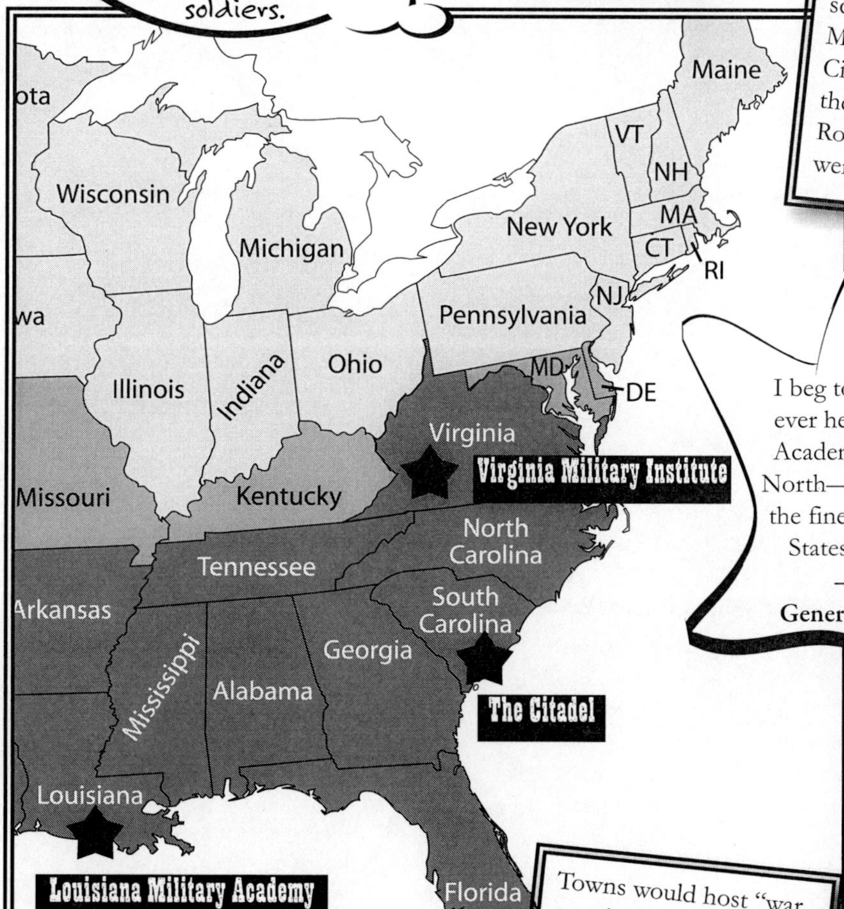

I beg to differ, Sir! By chance, have you ever heard of the United States Military Academy at West Point? Located in the North—New York, to be exact!—it's only the finest military academy in the United States! Why, I am a graduate myself!

—General Ulysses S. Grant, General-in-Chief, United States Army

Confederate General Thomas "Stonewall" Jackson was a graduate of West Point and later a professor at Virginia Military Institute!

Towns would host "war meetings" to coax their men to enlist in the army—with rousing, patriotic music and stirring testimonies of bravery and honor. Once the men enlisted, they were assigned to a company and sent off to training and battle!

The typical soldier on both sides was a white farmer in his early 20s. He was about 5'8" tall and weighed 143 pounds!

forms Female Anti-Slavery Society…Theodore Weld forms American Anti-Slavery Society…Ohio's Oberlin College 1st to admit blacks…1835… South Carolina

people organize to press their demands for justice… President Roosevelt issues an executive order against discrimination of workers in defense industries and government…1942… Margaret Walker wins the Yale Award for Young Poets for her

Where Did They FIGHT?

The Civil War was fought primarily in the South. To bring the South back into the Union, Northern troops had to invade the South. Fighting on familiar ground was an advantage for the Confederates. They knew the land—where to cross the river, where to hide in the woods, or where the back roads were located.

We'll make a pontoon bridge, Sir! We'll bring in wooden boats, set 'em side by side across the river, anchor 'em down, and tie 'em together. We'll lay planks over 'em, and lash 'em down. We'll add straw and sand and then get everybody across, even the horses and wagons, Sir!
—Union engineer known as a "pontonier"

Showdown at Sea! Union Naval blockades along the southern seacoast played an important role in the Civil War. Union ships blocked critical supplies from getting to the Confederacy, crippling its economy, and causing suffering for its citizens.

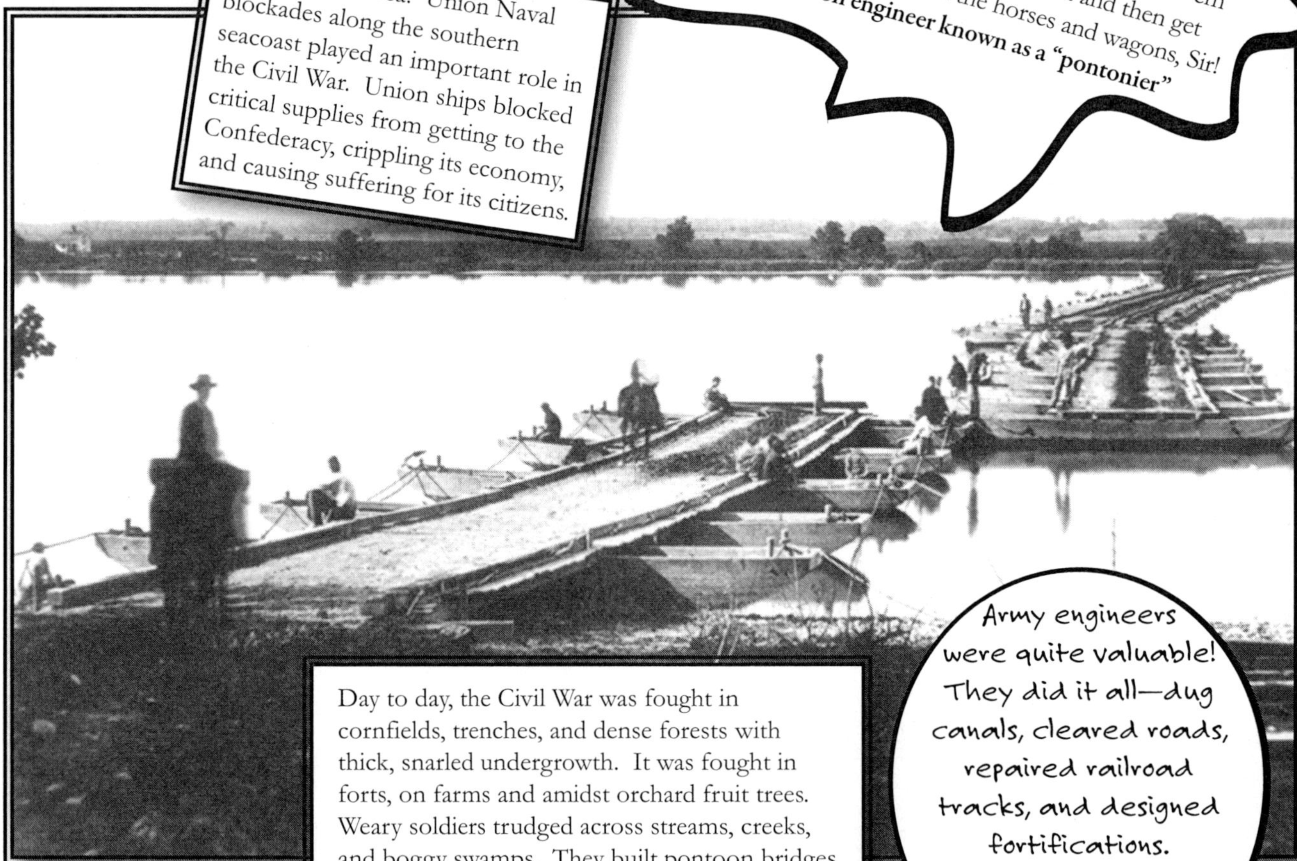

Day to day, the Civil War was fought in cornfields, trenches, and dense forests with thick, snarled undergrowth. It was fought in forts, on farms and amidst orchard fruit trees. Weary soldiers trudged across streams, creeks, and boggy swamps. They built pontoon bridges to get across rivers. They scrambled up and down ridges, valleys, and bluffs. Northerners and Southerners fought some battles by shooting cannons at a distance, while far too many others involved grisly, hand-to-hand "guerrilla" combat.

Army engineers were quite valuable! They did it all—dug canals, cleared roads, repaired railroad tracks, and designed fortifications. They even surveyed land to make maps!

Railroad Rumble! A battle on train tracks took place near Chattanooga, TN when Confederate troops stopped Union soldiers from stealing an important locomotive engine!

Southern homes were turned into military headquarters or makeshift hospitals while battles were fought on their lawns!

burns abolitionist literature...Georgia threatens to enact death penalty for abolitionist writers...Abolitionist William Ellery Channing publishes Slavery...1836

moving collection of poems, "For My People"...1947...Lawyer and economist, Sadie T.M. Alexander is appointed to Truman's Commission on Civil Rights...CORE sends its first group of "Freedom Riders" through the South...1948... President

Where Were Soldiers BURIED?

It's hard to imagine the task of burying thousands of bodies after many of the Civil War battles. After the Battle of Gettysburg, for example, more than 6,000 soldiers lay dead on the battlefield. What happened to them?

In many cases, the losing side retreated after the battle, leaving burials to be done by the winner. If the Union won the battle, the dead were usually buried somewhere on or near the battle site. The bodies might be buried in individual or mass graves. If pine boxes or coffins were available, they were used, but that was rare in the early years of the war.

It was common for soldiers who died in hospitals or camps to be buried in cemeteries. Families did their best to bring their loved one home for burial.

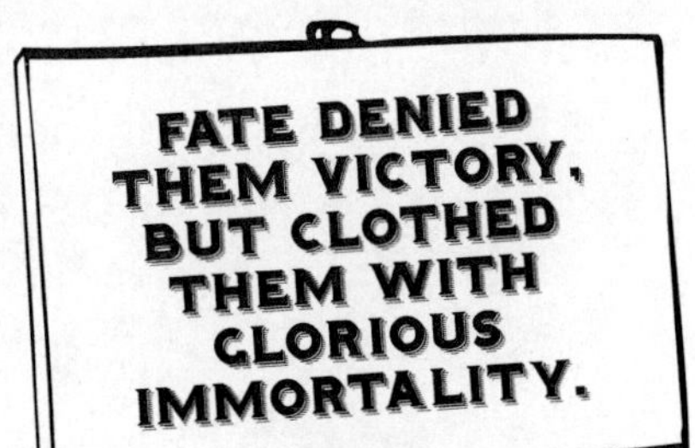

Sign at the Confederate Cemetery of Fredericksburg and Spotsylvania Court House

Congress approved the purchase of land for many military cemeteries to be located on or near major battlefields, like Gettysburg, Pennsylvania or Chattanooga, Tennessee. They are truly sacred places!

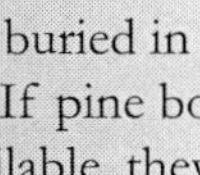

More than 618,000 Americans died in the Civil War.

Arlington National Cemetery near Washington, D.C. was established during the Civil War. It occupies land once owned by the family of Robert E. Lee's wife Mary Anna (Custis) Lee, a descendant of Martha Washington.

Where Was the First MAJOR BATTLE of the Civil War?

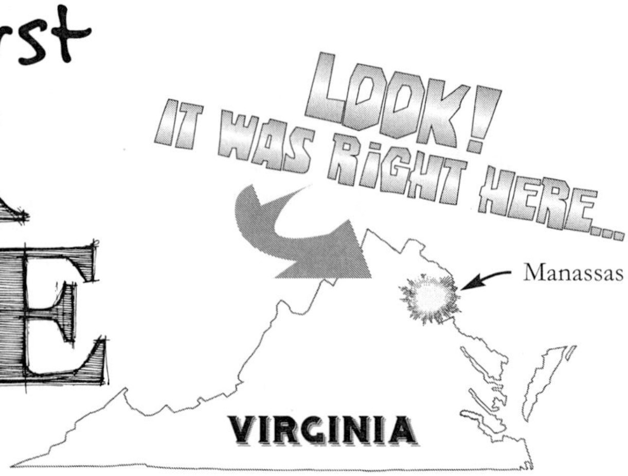

The first major battle of the Civil War occurred on July 21, 1861. It was fought at Manassas, Virginia, near a muddy stream known as Bull Run. Everyone in Washington, D.C. and the surrounding area had heard talk of troops gathering outside of town. Many citizens expected the Union troops to quickly defeat the Confederates. Buggies full of spectators with picnic baskets traveled to see the battle!

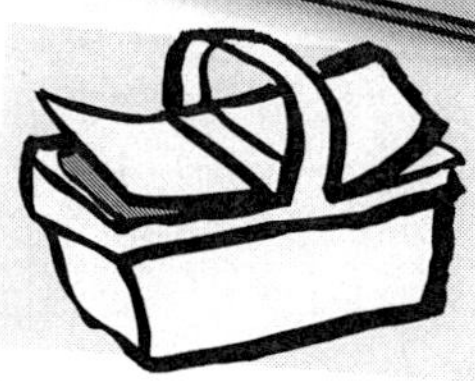

It didn't take long for them to realize that war is no picnic! The reality of the battlefield was torn limbs, agonizing screams, and the living picking the pockets of the dead. By afternoon, bodies littered the ground and neither side seemed to be winning. The tide turned once fresh Southern troops arrived. The Rebels attacked with bloodcurdling shouts they called the "Rebel yell." The South won the first Battle of Bull Run.

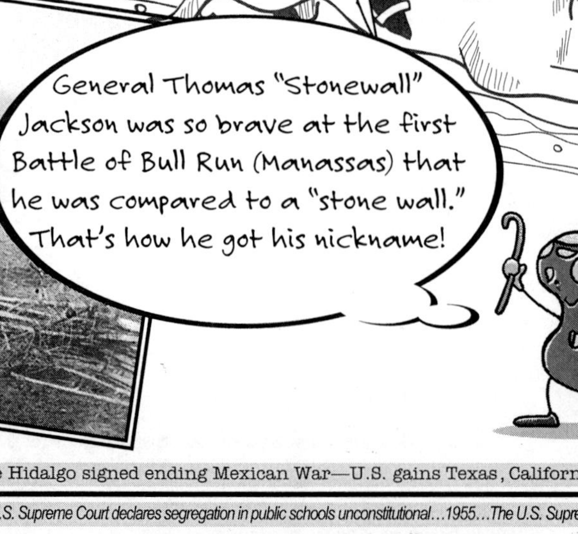

Where Were the SLAVES?

By 1860 the Southern economy was generating great wealth for the United States. Cotton exports were an important part of that income. And slaves were essential to keep that economic engine going!

Diagram of a plantation

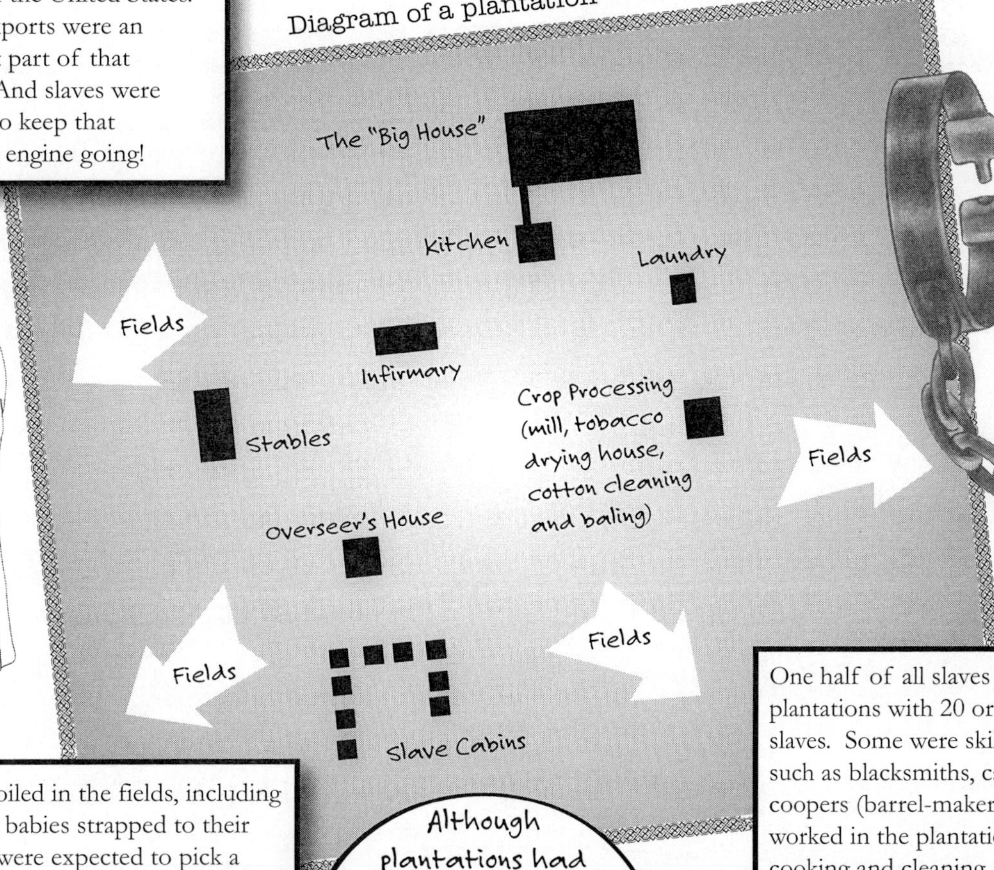

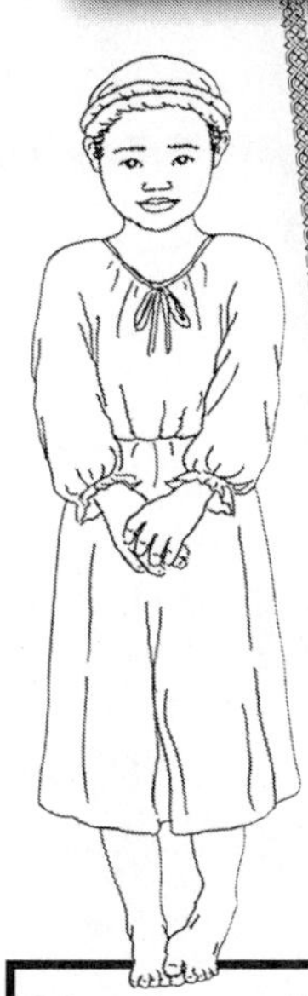

Most slaves toiled in the fields, including mothers with babies strapped to their backs. They were expected to pick a certain amount of cotton each day, and often punished if they failed. It was exhausting, backbreaking work.

One half of all slaves lived on plantations with 20 or more slaves. Some were skilled workers, such as blacksmiths, carpenters, or coopers (barrel-makers). Others worked in the plantation house, cooking and cleaning.

Although plantations had lots of slaves, the average slave owner in the South lived in a log cabin and only owned 4-5 slaves.

cotton fields

1850...Congress passes the Compromise of 1850...1852...Harriet Beecher Stowe publishes Uncle Tom's Cabin...1854...Congress passes the Kansas-Nebraska

deliberate speed."...In Montgomery, Alabama, Rosa Parks refuses to give up her seat on a public bus to a white man. She is arrested and jailed...A year-long bus boycott results in the U.S. Supreme Court invalidating segregation on Montgomery

Where Was the

UNDERGROUND RAILROAD?

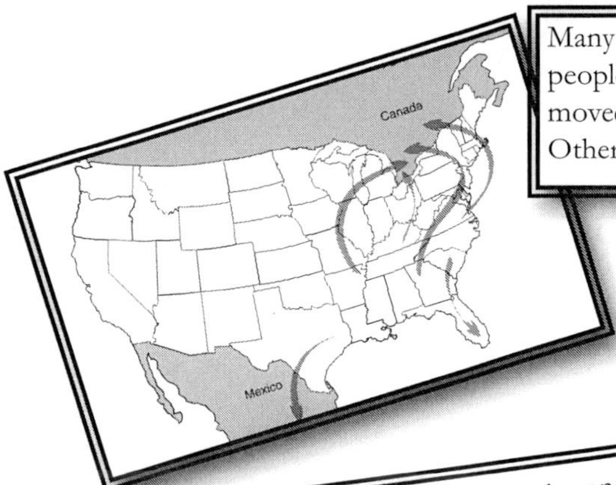

Many slaves in the South escaped to freedom through a secret network of people and places known as the Underground Railroad. "Conductors" moved slaves from slave states in the South to free states in the North. Others escaped to Mexico or islands in the Caribbean Sea.

My wife and I live in Indiana. We sometimes keep sick and hungry slaves in our home for weeks until they can travel again. We have a secret hiding place upstairs, and I have a wagon with a false bottom I use to transport them. Over 20 years, we have helped more than 2,000 runaways. May God bless every one of them. **—Levi Coffin**

Slaves hid in barns, tunnels, caves, wells, haystacks, and vegetable carts. They were rowed across deep rivers in the dead of night with only moonlight to guide them. They were fed and clothed by generous people along the way, who passed along secret messages to keep the slaves moving. Americans in more than 25 states took part in the Underground Railroad.

Escaping slaves often rubbed onions, bacon grease, or spruce gum on their feet to confuse the dogs tracking them. But the best way to throw them off was to go through water!

Act...1856...Proslavery candidate James Buchanan elected president...1857...Supreme Court rules escaped slave Dred Scott is property that must be returned

buses...1957...As president of the state NAACP, Daisy Gatson Bates leads the fight for school integration in Little Rock, Arkansas...1960...First student sit-ins at a lunch counter in Greensboro, North Carolina...1961...More than 50,000 people

Where Was the

INDUSTRIAL MIGHT?

Let's crunch the numbers...

- •90% of industrial goods were produced in the North
- •1.3 million people worked in factories in the North
- •110,000 people worked in factories in the South
- •North had 110,000 manufacturing companies
- •South had 18,000 manufacturing companies
- •North had more than 23,000 miles of railroad to transport goods
- •South had only 9,000 miles of railroad

The advantages of the industrial North were that they could crank out the "stuff" of war: cannons·rifles·ironclad ships·railroad engines ·shoes and boots

The South grew a lot of crops for food, but didn't have factories to can the food or railroads to distribute it.

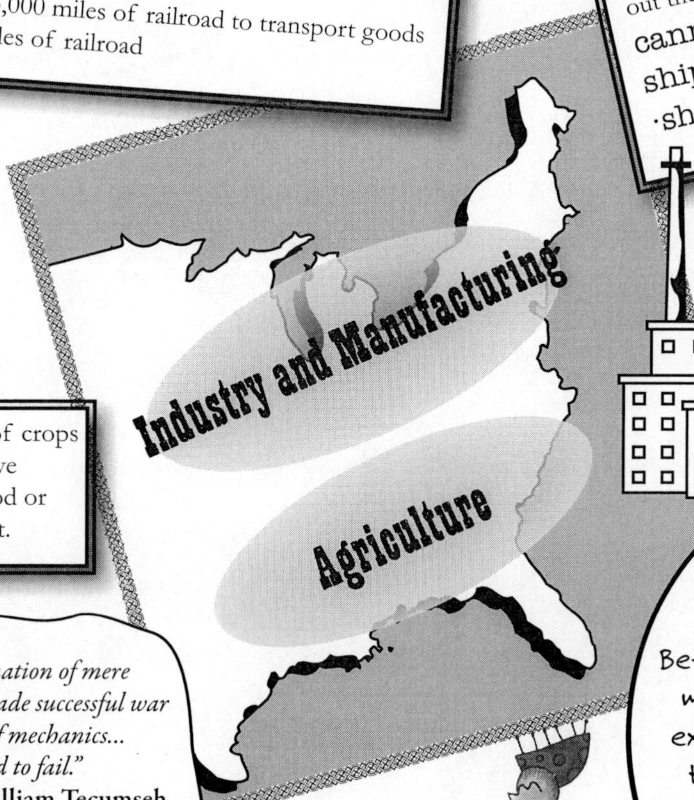

"In all history no nation of mere agriculturalists ever made successful war against a nation of mechanics... You are bound to fail."
—Union General William Tecumseh Sherman, in a letter to a Southern friend

The South's strength lay in land, slaves, and cotton. Before the Civil War, cotton made up half of all U.S. export earnings! Actually, the money from cotton exports had paid for many of the North's factories!

to owner...1858...Minnesota joins Union as free state...Illinois candidates Abraham Lincoln and Stephen Douglas debate issues of slavery; Douglas wins

demonstrate for equal rights in 100 cities, and over 3,600 are jailed...1963 ...Dr. Martin Luther King, Jr., delivers his "I Have a Dream" speech...Gloria Richardson is the only black woman to lead a local civil rights group... Charlayne Hunter-Gault is

Where (and What) Was the CAVALRY?

HEY! You said this horse could jump as high as a ten foot fence and he can't jump at all.

Well neither can a fence!

The cavalry is made up of soldiers on horseback. Early in the Civil War, the cavalry's primary role was to patrol, scout the enemy's advance, guard railroads carrying supplies, and escort generals. But as the war continued, the cavalry became a fearsome, mobile fighting force! Armed with pistols, sabers, and light automatic rifles known as carbines, cavalrymen often terrorized enemy foot soldiers!

It was important for cavalrymen to take good care of their horses. Union cavalry units had blacksmiths to shoe their horses and tend them in camp. If a horse got hurt, Union soldiers were usually able to get another one from a herd that traveled with the army. Southern soldiers usually brought their own horses with them from home and might end up as a foot soldier if their horse was injured!

The Confederate cavalry generally had faster horses than the Union. Southerners liked horse racing, so they bred their horses to be fast!

General Grant had three horses. They were named EGYPT, CINCINNATI, and the little one was JEFF DAVIS!

Confederate General Nathan Bedford Forrest was a skilled cavalry officer known as the "Wizard of the Saddle." Union General William Sherman wanted him to be hunted down and killed "if it costs 10,000 lives and bankrupts the Federal treasury."

I know my poor old horse is mighty tired, but we got to get back to camp fast! When I scouted today, I saw the enemy advancing 'cross Old Picket Creek. We didn't expect 'em to be comin' from that direction. I gotta tell the general!
—Louis Johnson, 7th Indiana Cavalry, 114th Regiment

Where Was the Most Famous NAVAL BATTLE?

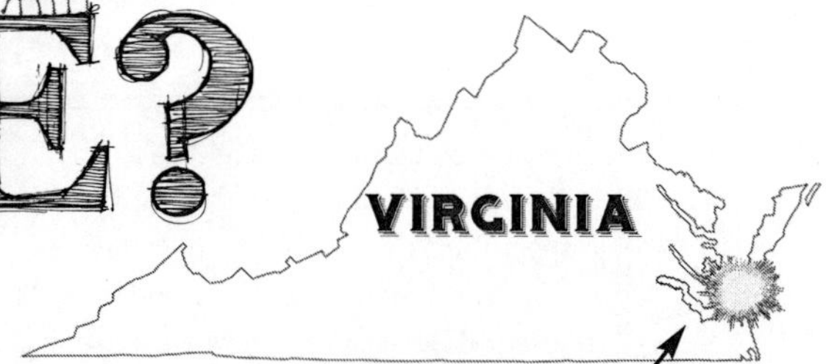

The waters off Hampton Roads, Virginia were the setting for the most famous naval battle of the Civil War between two ironclad warships!

It was no day at the beach!

The *Merrimack* was a wooden Union warship. The Confederates captured it, converted it into a ship with iron sides, and renamed it the *Virginia*. They were proud of their new invention! But—surprise! The Union had also created an ironclad vessel named the *Monitor*!

SPLOOSH!

In March 1862, the two vessels met for the first battle between ironclad warships. They battled for more than three hours. Their bullets had little effect on the ships, and the battle ended in a draw. Both sides now knew that wooden-hulled ships were on the way out, and they raced to produce more ironclad vessels!

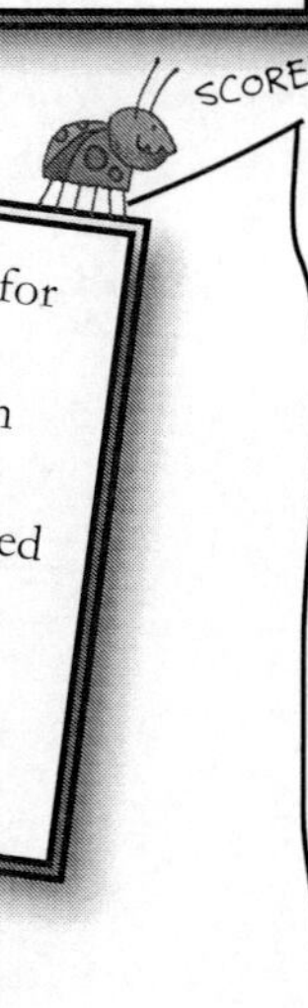

How did the Confederates get the *Merrimack* in the first place? After the war began, Union troops sank the ship when they evacuated the Navy yard at Portsmouth, Virginia. Confederate forces raised the ship and turned it into their ironclad treasure!

Where Was the BLOODIEST One-Day Battle?

It was a peaceful landscape of green, rolling hills and farmland dotted with forests—until September 17, 1862. On that day, the bloodiest one-day battle of the Civil War occurred between Antietam Creek and the town of Sharpsburg, Maryland.

As we appeared at the edge of the corn, a long line of men in butternut and gray rose up from the ground. Simultaneously, the hostile battle lines opened a tremendous fire upon each other. Men, I cannot say fell; they were knocked out of the ranks by dozens. **—Rufus Dawes, Union major, at the Battle of Antietam**

The Battle of Antietam was the first major Civil War battle on Northern soil. More than 23,000 men were killed, wounded, or went missing in a single day. The nation was shocked by the number of casualties! More soldiers were killed and wounded than the deaths of all Americans in the Revolutionary War+the War of 1812+theMexican War+ the Spanish-American War!

Really, the whole war was bloody!

The battle ended in a stalemate with no clear winner. Confederate General Robert E. Lee took his men back to Virginia, ending his invasion of the North.

Before the battle, General Lee's army was walking north through Maryland. His Confederate army was in need of something very important—shoes! Many Confederate soldiers were barefoot, and lagged behind because of it.

The North called this the Battle of Antietam, while the South called it the Battle of Sharpsburg.

See, I told you, shoes are important, tenderfoot!

Union...Kansas joins Union as free state...Southern states form Confederate States of America...Jefferson Davis elected Confederate president...Richmond

Mississippi...1965...Septima Poinsette Clark leads an Southern Christian Leadership Conference group which registers about 7,000 black voters in Alabama...Voting Rights Act allows blacks to vote freely and unhindered...1966...Black Panther

Where Were the CHILDREN?

Experts estimate that about 5% of Civil War soldiers were less than 18 years old! Although 17 was the youngest age anyone could enlist in the army during the war, children much younger sometimes lied about their ages, or hung around regiments until they were old enough to join. Boys as young as nine years old served as drummer boys!

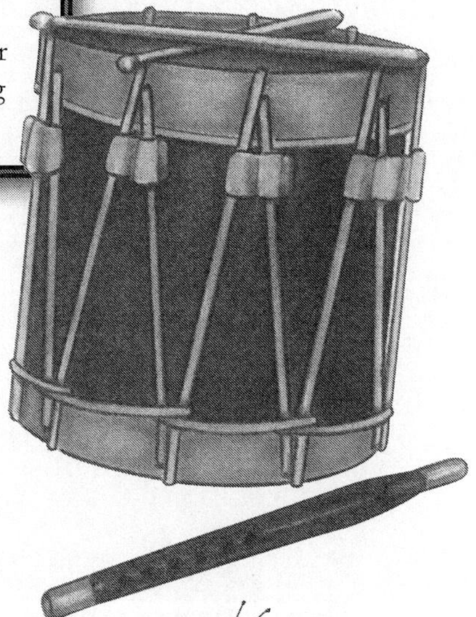

What about back home? Many children, particularly in the South, saw war close up. Many Northern children, away from the battle zone, spent time volunteering to help raise money for hospitals or soldiers' homes.

My fingers are sore but I am glad to do it. My brothers and I scraped lint from linen all day. My mother tells me they use the lint to pack into soldiers' wounds. I surely hope it helps them.
—Mary Sue, 9, Massachusetts

My pa's been gone a long time. We got 20 slaves and they'll do what I ask 'em. If they bring in the sugarcane, I'll grind it. My pa showed me how. I can do it.
—Benny, 12, Louisiana

They brought soldiers, moaning and crying, into our dining room. They turned over our piano and made it into a table to amputate arms and legs! It was the worst thing I'd ever seen.
—Emily, 14, Virginia

After the battle wuz over, them soldiers took it all; thar weren't a chicken nor a goose nor a year of corn to be found 'bout our place.
—Dell, 9, a Tennessee slave

Where Were IMPORTANT

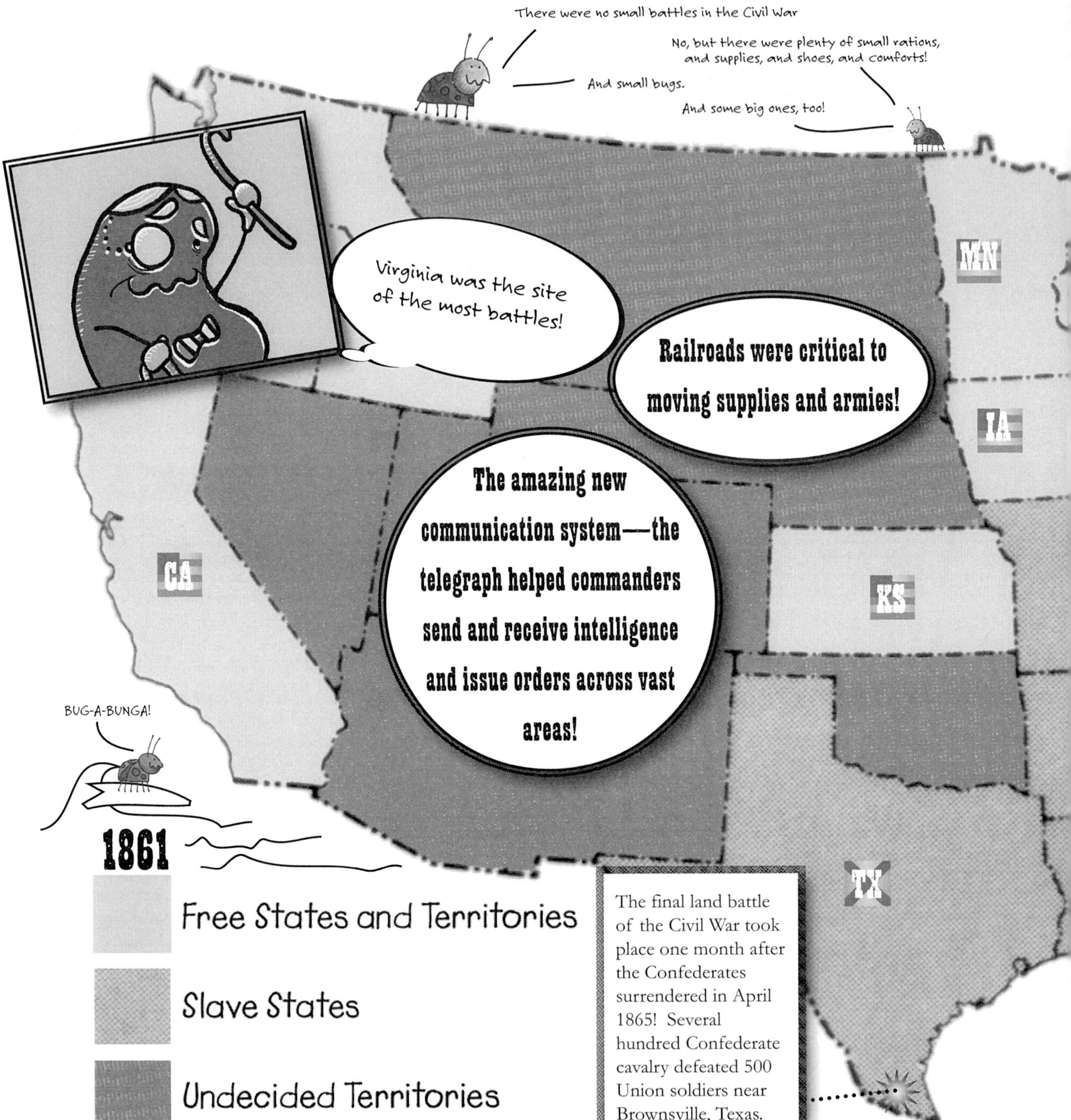

The final land battle of the Civil War took place one month after the Confederates surrendered in April 1865! Several hundred Confederate cavalry defeated 500 Union soldiers near Brownsville, Texas.

officially begins…Federal Navy blockades Southern ports…Virginia, Arkansas, North Carolina, and Tennessee join Confederacy…Union defeated at Battle of

York elects Shirley Chisholm as first African American U.S. Congresswoman…1969…Mary Moultrie leads a wage strike at the Medical College Hospital in South Carolina...1972… Political activist and intellectual, Angela Davis is acquitted of murder

BATTLES of the Civil War?

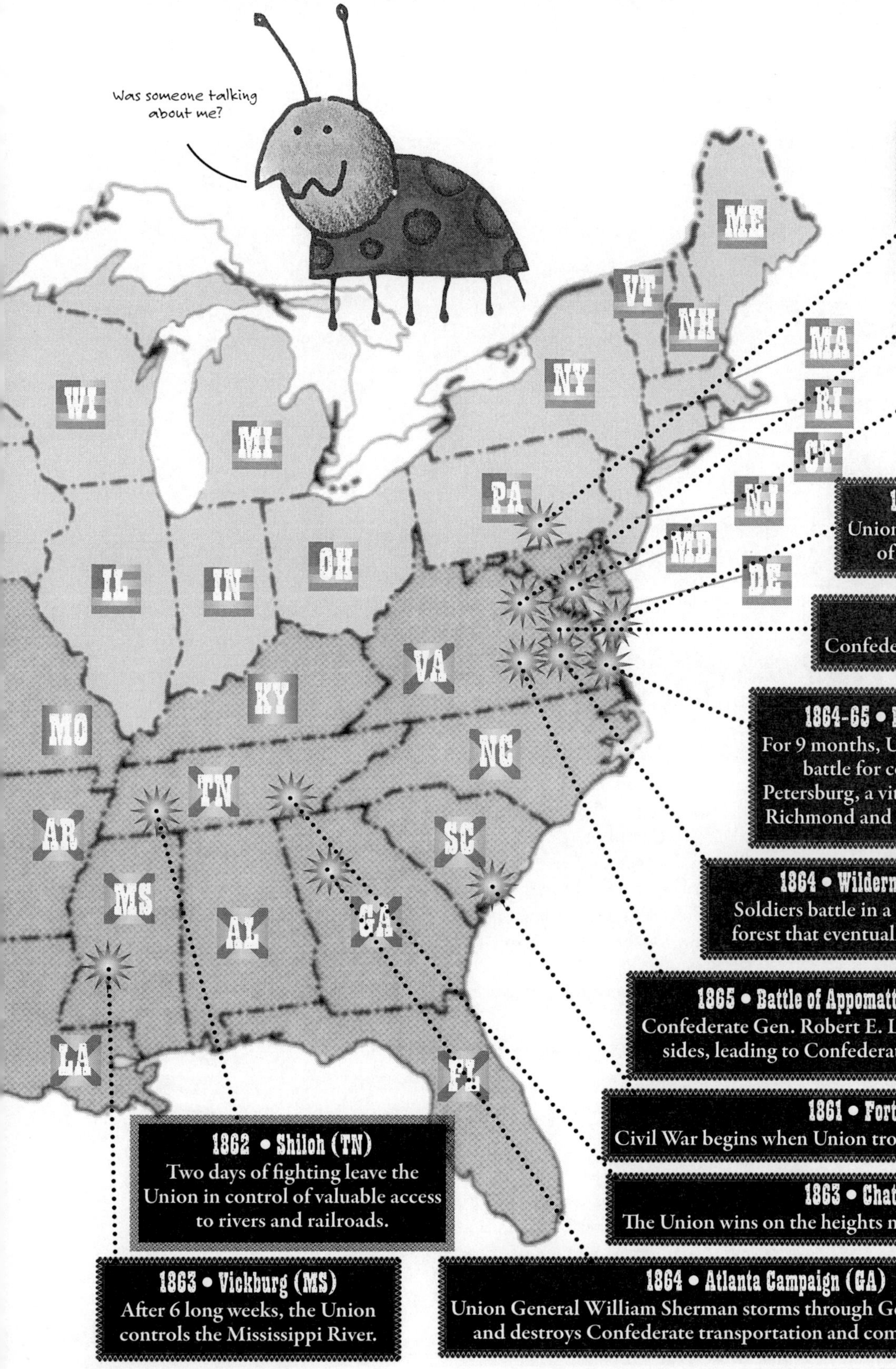

1863 • Gettysburg (PA)
The Union is victor in this turning point of the war!

1861 • first Battle of Bull Run (VA)
Also called Manassas; 1st major land battle!

1862 • Antietam (MD)
Bloodiest one-day battle of the Civil War!

1862 • Peninsula Campaign (VA)
Union troops advance within a few miles of Richmond but are driven back.

1862 • Fredericksburg (VA)
Confederate troops force a decisive victory!

1864-65 • Petersburg Campaign (VA)
For 9 months, Union and Confederate forces battle for control of Richmond and Petersburg, a vital railroad junction. Finally, Richmond and Petersburg fall to the Union.

1864 • Wilderness (VA)
Soldiers battle in a thick, tangled forest that eventually catches fire!

1865 • Battle of Appomattox Court House (VA)
Confederate Gen. Robert E. Lee is surrounded on three sides, leading to Confederate surrender on April 9.

1861 • Fort Sumter (SC)
Civil War begins when Union troops surrender to the Confederates!

1863 • Chattanooga (TN)
The Union wins on the heights north and east of this strategic city.

1862 • Shiloh (TN)
Two days of fighting leave the Union in control of valuable access to rivers and railroads.

1863 • Vickburg (MS)
After 6 long weeks, the Union controls the Mississippi River.

1864 • Atlanta Campaign (GA)
Union General William Sherman storms through Georgia, burns Atlanta, and destroys Confederate transportation and communications hubs.

Bull Run—first official battle of the Civil War...1862...1st ironclad ship battle between Monitor and Merrimac...2nd Battle of Bull Run ends in Union defeat

in a political trial in California... Equal Employment Opportunity Act passes...1974...The Coalition of Labor Union Women is formed...1978...U.S. Postal Service issues a Black Heritage postage stamp series...1983...Martin Luther King, Jr. Day is

Where Did Soldiers SLEEP?

This is for the dogs!

Where a Civil War soldier laid his head for the night depended on where he was and the time of year. Except in the winter, Union soldiers typically slept in tents. The most common type of tent was a two-man tent known as a "dog tent." It was two rectangular pieces of canvas buttoned together. Soldiers set up the tent by tying each end to a stick or a rifle stuck in the ground by the bayonet.

Zzzz

Most Confederate soldiers did not have shelter tents so they captured Union tents whenever possible. Confederate camps were often filled with Union prizes like tents, blankets, canteens, and haversacks, small canvas bags used to carry food. Confederates often simply slept under the starry skies!

Your snoring kept me awake last night!

Are you sure it wasn't canon-fire, bugs, heat, rain, racoons in your rations or that pinecone you used as a pillow?

No. You snore REALLY loud!

Welcome to the SCARY-OTT! May I show you to your mud-hole?

In the winter, soldiers built log huts that looked like frontier cabins. They named them after fancy hotels or put up signs like: The Hole in the Wall or The Swine Hotel. Others put tents on log bases and kept water out (sort of!) by stretching rubber blankets or ponchos over the top.

Gonna take a bath today in the river over there. Gonna feel great! Then I'm gonna wash my clothes too and string 'em out over a tree to dry. It'll feel so good to be clean after a month of dirt!
—Union private

The "dog tent" got its name because soldiers joked that "only a dog could crawl under it and stay dry from the rain!"

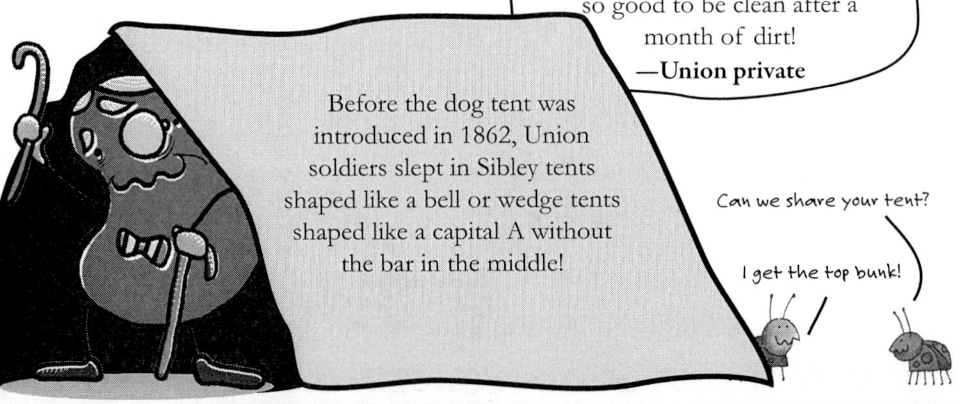

Before the dog tent was introduced in 1862, Union soldiers slept in Sibley tents shaped like a bell or wedge tents shaped like a capital A without the bar in the middle!

It was "RUFF!"

So are your jokes!

Can we share your tent?

I get the top bunk!

...Battle of Antietam becomes bloodiest day of the Civil War...1st black regiment formed...1863...President Lincoln issues Emancipation Proclamation...Union

first celebrated on January 20th as a federal holiday...1989...General Colin Powell chosen as first black chairman of Joint Chiefs of Staff, the nation's top military position...1991... Civil Rights Act limits affirmative action...1992...Mae Jemison

PRISONS? Where were the

More than 400,000 soldiers were sent to about 150 Union and Confederate prison camps during the Civil War. In general, they were horrible! Of the 20-25 major prisons, the two most notorious were the Confederate prison at Andersonville, Georgia, and the Union prison in Elmira, New York.

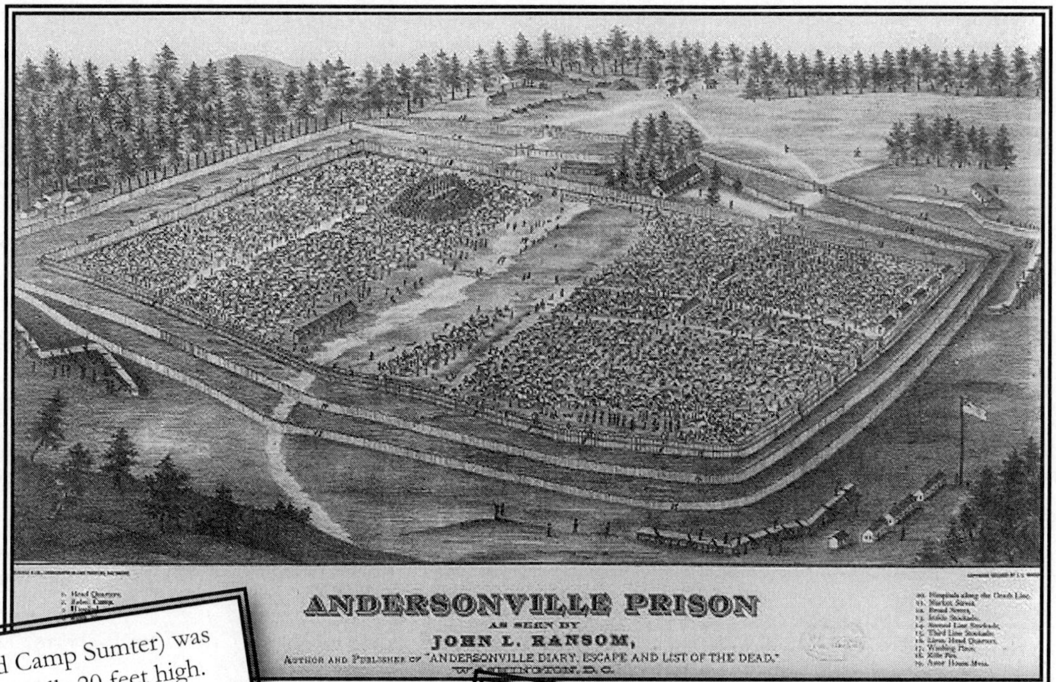

Andersonville (officially named Camp Sumter) was an open pen surrounded by log walls 20 feet high. Thousands of men crowded together, with the only bathroom a foul, polluted stream running through the camp. There were no barracks, so prisoners suffered through cold winter rains and scorching summer heat with no shelter. Many prisoners were skinny as skeletons because there was little food to eat. Almost 1/3 of the 45,000 prisoners at Andersonville died in camp.

Similar conditions existed at Elmira, except that some barracks and tents were available. But even those weren't enough for one especially cold winter, when 1/4 of prisoners died from exposure.

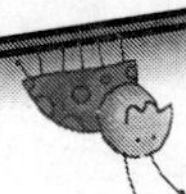

About 56,000 prisoners died in Civil War prison camps. That number almost equals the number of soldiers who died in the Vietnam War 100 years later!

I Don't Think Thar is any Place in Hell Hot Anuf for Thos 3 men.
—Tennessee prisoner at Fort Delaware prison, Delaware, talking about cruel guards

War Department establishes Bureau of Colored Troops...Confederate General Thomas "Stonewall" Jackson killed... Grant conquers Vicksburg, Mississippi

becomes the first African American female U.S. astronaut...1993...Toni Morrison becomes first African American female to win a Pulitzer Prize in literature for her novel, Beloved...2000...President George W. Bush appoints African American

What About FORTS and FORTIFICATIONS?

Many Civil War battles involved forts or fortifications. A fortification is anything that protects soldiers from fire. Many forts were part of a string built along the Atlantic coast after the War of 1812. These forts were built at strategic locations. Examples include Fort Sumter in Charleston Harbor in South Carolina, and Fort Pulaski on a Savannah River island in Georgia. Other forts were built inland as river defenses like Fort Donelson in Tennessee.

Both Union and Confederate commanders used fortifications to protect their soldiers.

•A blockhouse was a simple log building. Soldiers fired rifles through small openings in the walls.

•Breastworks were chest-high barricades made of logs and dirt.

•Trenches were long, narrow ditches dug in the ground.

The Battle of Vicksburg involved fortifications built by both sides. Confederates built nine miles of sturdy defenses to protect the city. "We'll have to dig our way in," said General Grant. So the Union built miles of earthworks themselves, settling in for a six-week siege that ended in a Union victory in July 1863!

...Union gains control of Mississippi River...West Virginia joins Union as free state...Battle of Gettysburg begins to turn tide of war for Union... Lincoln gives

Condoleezza Rice to serve as his U.S. National Security Advisor...2002...Tiger Woods becomes the youngest golfer (age 26!) to win 8 PGA major titles...African American tennis star Serena Williams wins the U.S. Open and Wimbledon

Where Did They Take the WOUNDED?

About a mile behind the front lines of a battle was a very important place—the field hospital. It might be a building like a church or barn, but it was just as likely to be a clearing in the woods or a farmer's front yard. The field hospital was a place of pain and commotion. Men screamed and begged for help while one or two surgeons worked frantically to help them. A wooden door or boards laid across barrels often served as operating tables.

Oh boy! When they said "field hospital," they meant FIELD hospital!

All the cow-houses, wagon-sheds, hay-barracks, hen-coops, Negro cabins, and barns were turned into hospitals.
—reporter for the New York Herald, about the Peninsula Campaign

Ambulance wagons removed wounded from the battlefield. The ride could be horribly rough and painful. To take the wounded to hospitals, the Union set up special train cars and hospital ships like the Navy's Red Rover.

Red Rover, Red Rover, send wounded soldiers right over. (And some bandages, too!)

Twice as many soldiers died from disease than from bullets during the Civil War!

Ouch!

After the Battle of Gettysburg, Confederate General Robert E. Lee left with a wagon train of wounded that stretched for 17 miles!

Gettysburg Address...Union forces gain control Tennessee...1864...Grant appointed commander of Union Army...General Sherman conquers Atlanta, Georgia

tournaments...Talk show host Oprah Winfery receives the first Bob Hope Humanitarian Award at the 54th Annual Emmy Awards...Halle Berry becomes first African American to win an Academy Award for best actress...The Slavery Reparations

Where Was the "MARCH TO THE SEA"?

The year of 1864 brought bad times to the South, especially Georgia. Union General William Tecumseh Sherman's Atlanta Campaign was one of death and destruction. He moved his army south from Tennessee into Atlanta, fighting Confederate soldiers along the way. When the Union troops finally took over Atlanta, they set the city on fire!

Atlanta Railroad station before Sherman's Atlanta campaign...

...and after!

I prefer marching to band music!

In November, Sherman's troops left Atlanta. They split into two groups and headed to Savannah on the Atlantic coast. This journey is called the "March to the Sea." Along the way, Union troops destroyed homes, stores, crops, bridges, and railroad tracks. Sherman was trying to crush any fighting spirit left in the South. He did a good job.

To my smoke-house, my dairy, pantry, kitchen, and cellar, like famished wolves they come, breaking locks and whatever is in their way. The thousand pounds of meat in my smoke-house is gone in a twinkling, my flour, my meat, my lard, butter, eggs, pickles of various kinds—both in vinegar and brine—wine, jars, and jugs are all gone. My eighteen fat turkeys, my hens, chickens, and fowls, my young pigs, are shot down in my yard and hunted as if they were rebels themselves. **—Dolly Sumner Lunt, Georgia plantation mistress**

On their way to Atlanta, Union troops tore up railroad tracks. They built bonfires and wrapped red-hot rails around trees, calling them "Sherman's neckties."

Sherman and his army reached Savannah just before Christmas. He sent President Lincoln a telegram presenting the city as a Christmas gift!

But what Lincoln really wanted was an MP3 player!

...Maryland abolishes slavery...Nevada joins union as free state...Abraham Lincoln wins reelection as president...Sherman begins "March to the Sea" through

Coordinating Committee, led by prominent African American lawyers and activists, announce plans to sue companies that profited from slavery... President George W. Bush awards comedian and actor Bill Cosby and baseball player Hank Aaron

Where's My MAP?

At the beginning of the Civil War, few reliable maps were available for both Union and Confederate officers. Since knowing the terrain ahead was so important, topographic engineers began traveling with the army to make maps.

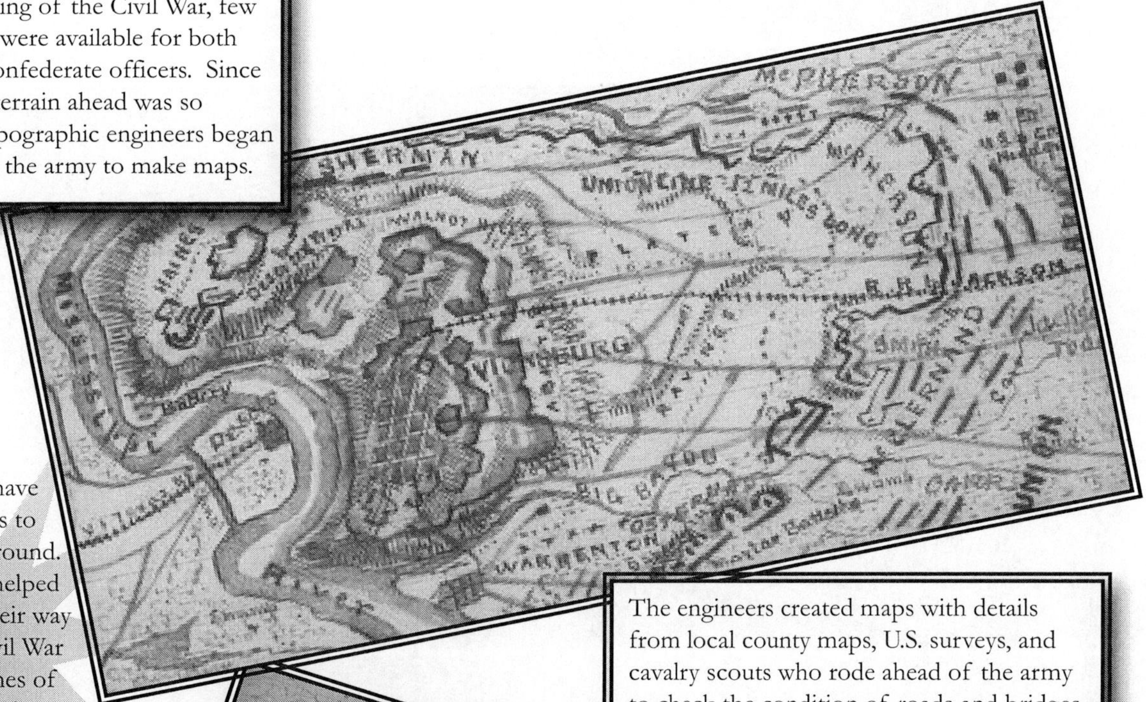

Today we have road names to help us get around. Details that helped people find their way around in Civil War included names of mills, schools, farmers, or taverns.

The engineers created maps with details from local county maps, U.S. surveys, and cavalry scouts who rode ahead of the army to check the condition of roads and bridges, locations of food and water, and natural defensive positions of the land. They also got information about the terrain from spies, prisoners, and local residents. The data was quickly transferred to maps made right in the field!

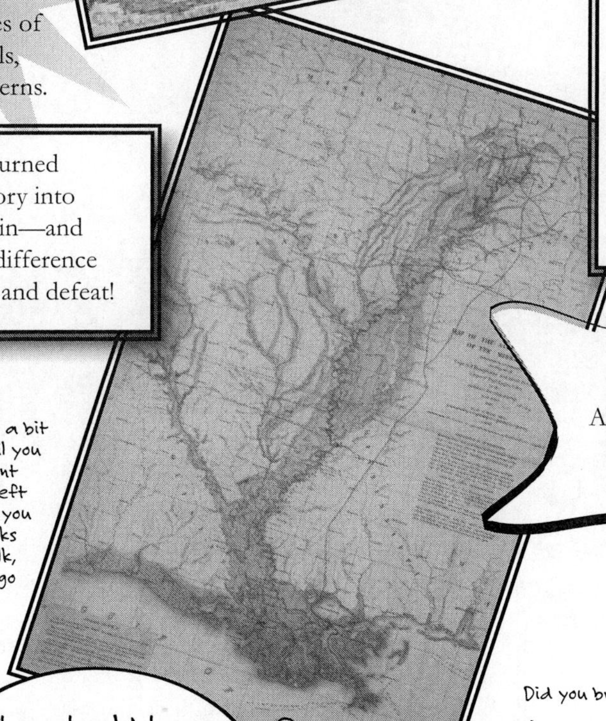

Accurate maps turned unfamiliar territory into predictable terrain—and often made the difference between victory and defeat!

General Sherman wants a map of Georgia, and he wants it fast! The Atlanta Campaign will be underway in just two days, and we've got to get cracking! **—Union topographical engineer**

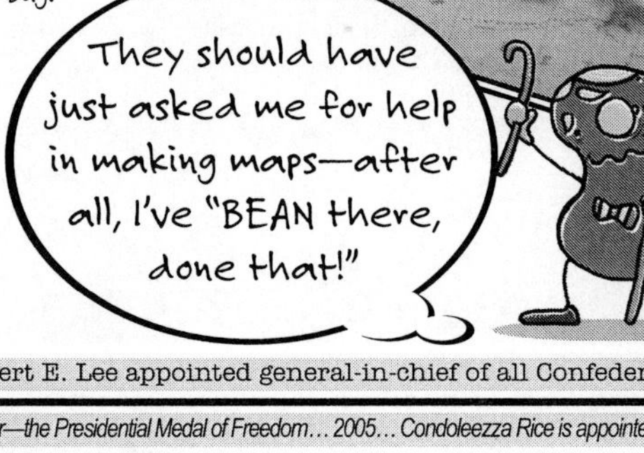

Georgia…1865…Robert E. Lee appointed general-in-chief of all Confederate armies…Missouri abolishes slavery…Abraham Lincoln rejects Jefferson Davis's

the nation's highest civilian honor—the Presidential Medal of Freedom… 2005… Condoleezza Rice is appointed Secretary of State becoming the first African American woman to serve as Secretary of State…Hurricane Katrina hits southern coast

Where Did the Civil War END?

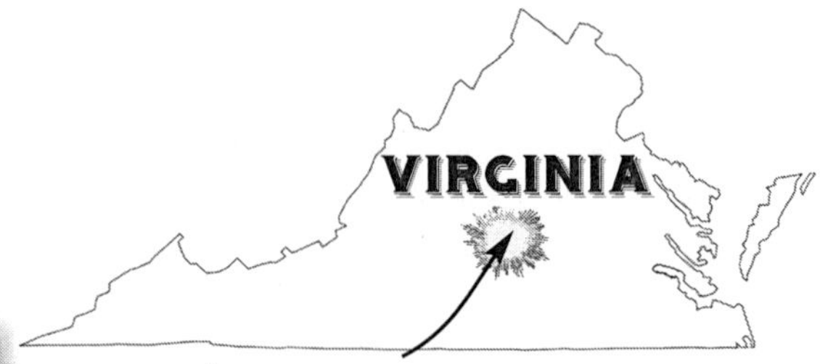

On April 9, 1865, General Robert E. Lee surrendered the Confederate forces to Union General Ulysses S. Grant at Appomattox Court House, Virginia.

Lee surrenders at Appomattox Court House

A grocer named Wilmer McLean owned the three-story home where the surrender took place. McLean had moved there after an artillery shell destroyed the chimney of his home in Manassas, Virginia during the Battle of Bull Run! Apparently, the war was following him!

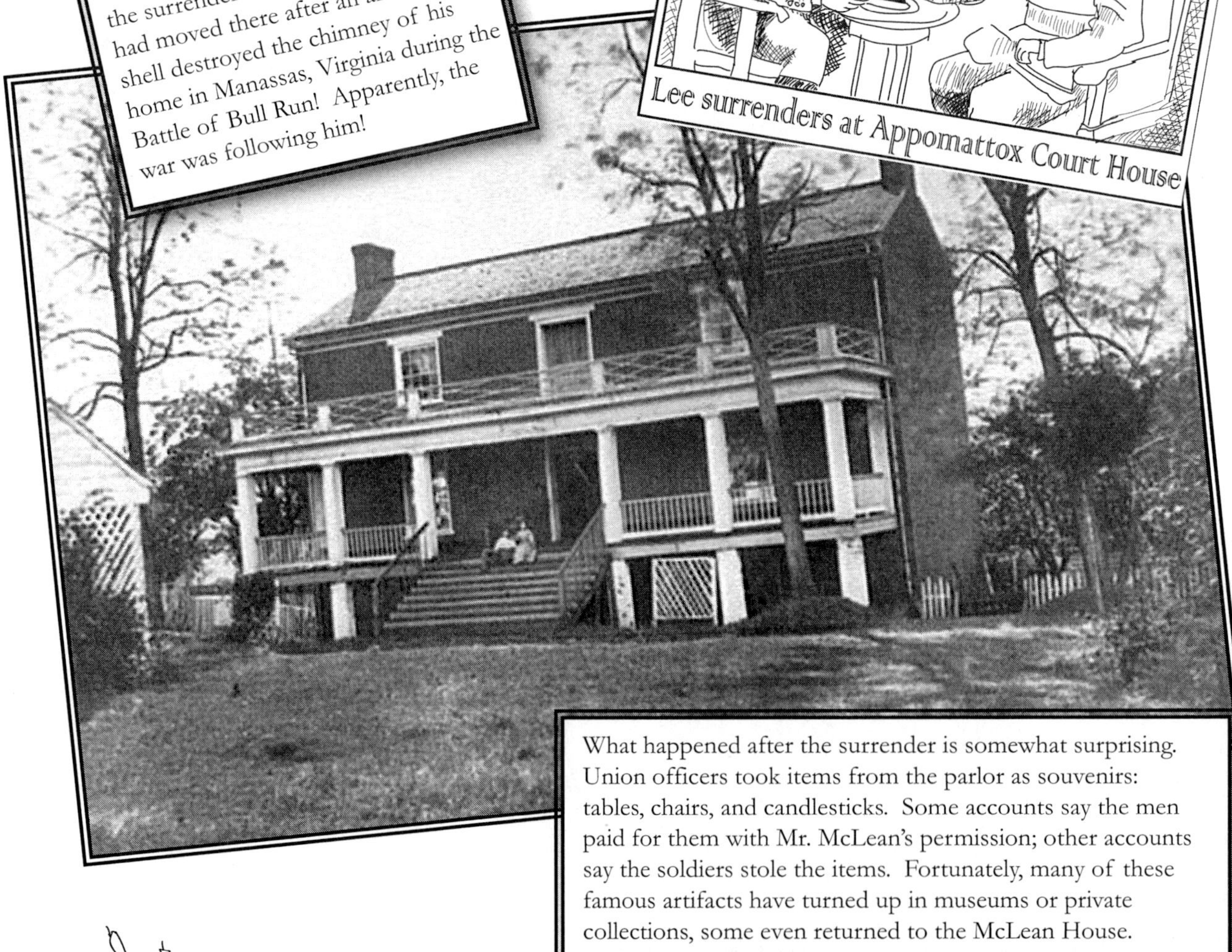

What happened after the surrender is somewhat surprising. Union officers took items from the parlor as souvenirs: tables, chairs, and candlesticks. Some accounts say the men paid for them with Mr. McLean's permission; other accounts say the soldiers stole the items. Fortunately, many of these famous artifacts have turned up in museums or private collections, some even returned to the McLean House.

peace proposals...13th Amendment to Constitution abolishes slavery...Confederates forced into full retreat...Confederate general Robert E. Lee surrenders to

of the United States...Ceremonial groundbreaking of the African Burial Ground in Manhattan takes place—the site will serve as memorial to 17th-18th century African slaves...Forbes magazine ranks Condoleezza Rice as the most powerful

Please Preserve the Sites!

Gettysburg. No shopping centers, please!

Civil War battlefields have long stood as silent witnesses to the most devastating war in American history. Today, many face a new enemy—the growth of nearby neighborhoods and businesses that threatens to swallow up precious, historic land.

The Civil War Preservation Trust watches over these sites. Each year, they publish a list of the 10 most endangered Civil War battlefields. Current endangered examples include Cedar Creek and the Wilderness in Virginia, and Gettysburg in Pennsylvania.

Cedar Creek Battlefield with reenactors and limestone mines!

What's happening to these battlefields? The Cedar Creek Battlefield faces a limestone mining operation across parts of the historic site. A giant superstore might be built just 1/4 mile from the Wilderness Battlefield. At Gettysburg, a group is seeking approval to build a gambling casino about 1/2 mile from the historic national park.

Why should we preserve Civil War battlefields? These battles changed American history (and possibly world history!) and are part of our national heritage. Preserving these sacred places helps us learn from the men who fought there, appreciate the freedoms they won, and honor their memories.

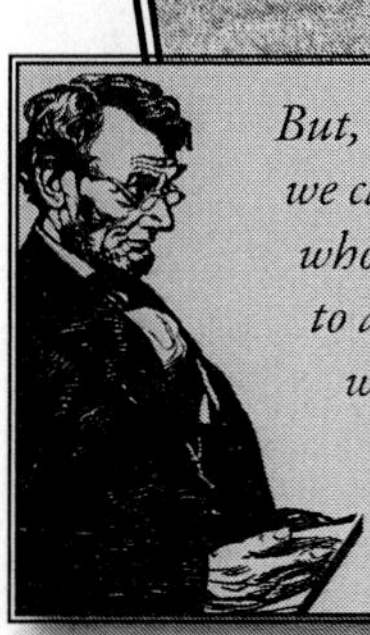

But, in a larger sense, we cannot dedicate—we cannot consecrate—we cannot hallow—this ground. The brave men, living and dead, who struggled here, have consecrated it, far above our poor power to add or detract. The world will little note, nor long remember what we say here, but it can never forget what they did here.

—President Abraham Lincoln, excerpt from the Gettysburg Address

If you want to help preserve Civil War parks, visit the Civil War Preservation Trust's website: www.civilwar.org.

I'm going there now!

Wait for me!

Civil War Gazetteer of Cool Names!

Antietam—creek in Virginia; from the Algonquian Indian language, perhaps meaning "swift water"

Appomattox—referring to the area where the Civil War surrender took place in 1865; from an Indian term meaning "tobacco plant country"

Bull Run—name of a creek in northeast Virginia

Chickamauga—creek in northwest Georgia; from Cherokee language, meaning "river of death" or "dwelling place of the war chief"

Chickahominy—Virginia river named after an Indian tribe

Devil's Den—landmark with granite formations and steep cliffs; provided protection for Union battery during Battle of Gettysburg in 1863

Five Forks—critical intersection in Virginia and site of Confederate loss in 1865

Little Round Top—smaller of two rocky hills south of Gettysburg, Pennsylvania

Manassas—Virginia town near Bull Run Creek

Potomac—river that flows into Chesapeake Bay, Virginia; from Indian language, meaning "great trading place"

Rappahannock—Virginia river; from Indian language, meaning "stream with an ebb and flow" or "river of quick-rising water"

Savage's Station—Virginia location of the fourth battle of the Seven Days' Battles in 1862

Totopotomoy—creek in Virginia; site of 1864 battle

Yazoo—river in Mississippi; 29 sunken Civil War ships lie beneath the river's waters

A Civil War "Where" Glossary

abatis: a fortification made of trees cut down so that their branches face the enemy

artillery: large guns like mortars and cannons (units armed with these guns were also referred to as "artillery")

battery: an artillery unit with 70-100 men and 4-6 large guns

blockade: a war measure that blocks ports and keeps ships from coming in or going out

breastworks: chest-high fortifications made of dirt and wood

cavalry: troops that ride horses into battle

earthworks: fortifications made of dirt

fort: strong or fortified place for protection against the enemy

fortification: works erected to defend a place

infantry: soldiers who are trained and equipped to fight on foot

lunette: a small two- or three-sided structure that faced away from the enemy

mortar: short, stubby cannons used for tossing bombs into fortifications

parapet: a low wall built to protect troops

rampart: a steeply sloped, earthen, wall-like ridge topped by a parapet

redan: a form of angled breastworks shaped like a V with its point facing the enemy

trench: a long, narrow ditch in the ground

Battlefields to visit

Antietam National Battlefield (PA)
Appomattox Court House National Historical Park (VA)
Brices Cross Roads National Battlefield Site (MS)
Chickamauga and Chattanooga National Military Park (GA; TN)
Fort Pulaski National Monument (GA)
Fort Sumter National Monument (SC)
Fort Donelson National Battlefield (TN; KY)
Fredericksburg and Spotsylvania County Battlefields Memorial National Military Park (VA)
Gettysburg National Military Park (PA)
Harpers Ferry National Historical Park (VA)
Kennesaw Mountain National Battlefield Park (GA)
Manassas National Battlefield (VA)
Monocacy National Battlefield (VA)
Pea Ridge National Military Park (MO)
Pecos National Historical Park (Glorieta Pass Battlefield) (NM)
Petersburg National Battlefield (VA)
Richmond National Battlefield Park (VA)
Shiloh National Military Park (TN)
Stones River National Battlefield (TN)
Tupelo National Battlefield (MS)
Vicksburg National Military Park (MS)
Wilson's Creek National Battlefield (MO)

Reconstruction

Reconstruction: the recovery and rebuilding period following the Civil War

Can you believe the war is finally over? The weight of the world has been lifted from my husband's shoulders. I can see it in his eyes. And we are going to Ford's Theatre to see a play tonight! A night of lighthearted fun—I cannot wait!—**Mary Todd Lincoln**

POP! What was that? Part of the play? Women are shrieking! A man has leaped onto the stage, yelled, and run off. The president slumps in his chair! I see blood! Can it be true?! Did someone just shoot our president?!—**usher**, Ford's Theatre

Stop that man!—**Major Henry Rathbone**

Everyone is sobbing. Our president died early this morning. May God have mercy on this country.—**newspaper reporter**

I accept this office of President of the United States with a heavy heart.—Vice President **Andrew Johnson**

He was in that barn and wouldn't come out. So we set it on fire! I saw my chance, and took it. I shot him. I shot and killed that John Wilkes Booth.—**Union soldier***

*The manhunt for John Wilkes Booth was the largest in history, involving 10,000 federal troops, detectives, and police.

Here are the latest statistics, Sir: 618,000 soldiers dead; probably 100,000 civilians killed too, Sir. That includes the North and South, Sir. And we know that disease killed twice as many as those who died in battle.—**Union soldier** *

*The Civil War death toll is more than the total killed in battle in the American Revolution, War of 1812, Mexican War, Spanish-American War, World War I, World War II, Korean War, Vietnam, and Gulf War—all combined!

The Legend of *Taps*

In 1862, Union Army Captain Robert Ellicombe looked over the battle scene. He heard the groan of a wounded soldier. Although, he did not know if the soldier was a Union soldier or a Confederate soldier, the captain crawled through the battle amidst gunfire and carried the soldier to the medical tent. When he got back, he found that the soldier was a Confederate, but he was already dead. He recognized the face of the soldier and realized it was his own son. Because the son was a Rebel, he was not allowed to have a full military burial. Only one musician, a bugler, was allowed to play. The father asked the bugler to play a song that was found in the pocket of his son's uniform. The bugler played the song that became known as *Taps*.

This story is legend, not historically accurate

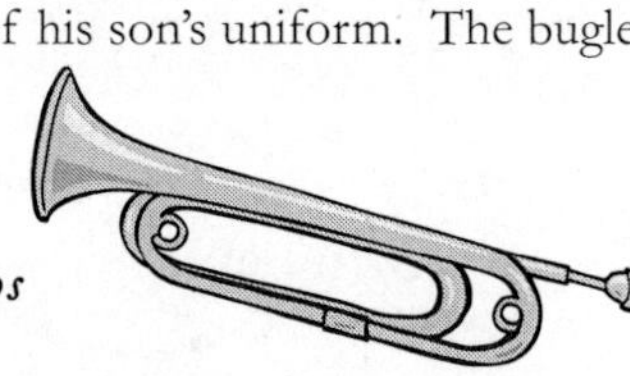

The True Story of *Taps*

General Daniel Butterfield was dissatisfied with the customary firing of three rifles at the end of military burials. He altered a French bugle call into what is now known as *Taps*. The song became very popular, and within months it was sounded by both the Union and Confederate armies.

This story is the true story of *Taps*. Not as fun and romantic as the Legend!

When we said our vows years ago, I was just a child. Jefferson was 18 years my elder. My momma almost cried when I said I wanted to marry him. But we've had a happy life together. Full of struggles, I suppose, but happy. I never thought I'd be the First Lady of the Confederacy, not in a million years! But I stand by Jefferson in everything. Right now he's locked up, accused of treason since the great South lost this Civil War. But I'm staying right here outside his jail cell. I'll fight for his release until I feel him back in my arms again, no matter how long it takes.—**Varina Howell Davis***

*Jefferson Davis was released in 1867 thanks to his wife's unrelenting requests for his freedom.

Everything is destroyed! Houses burned. Fields barren. Animals dead or dying—I can count their ribs. What has happened to our beautiful South?—**Confederate soldier**

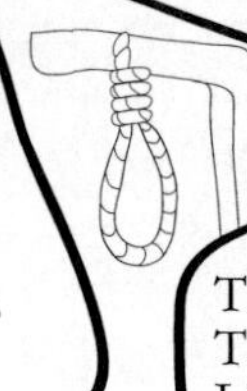

My lifeless body hangs on the scaffold. Three guilty men wave in the wind beside me. They accused me of conspiring to kill Abraham Lincoln. I did no such thing!—ghost of **Mary Surratt**

If these old walls could talk, they would tell a history so fascinating and terrifying, no student would ever tire of learning about American events. I was built years ago, before any of these men were even born. My walls were erected for protection, but just look at them now. Spirits seem to haunt this sad and forlorn place, and will forever more.—**Fort Monroe**

Did I ever think I would see this day? No, sir! No more slavery—thanks to the Thirteenth Amendment to the Constitution. What a day, what a day! Free at last! Praise the Lord!—**former slave**

We've got to keep these free blacks under control! We'll wear white robes and hoods and terrorize them at night—they'll think we're spirits of Confederate soldiers! That'll keep them in their place.—**Ku Klux Klan member***

* The Ku Klux Klan was a secret society organized by Southerners that used violence and terror to maintain "white supremacy."

I thought the war was over! But they passed that Military Reconstruction Act and Union troops are still here—occupying the South! It's like pouring salt into a fresh wound. And those Northerners wonder why we're bitter?!—**Southern schoolteacher**

Carpetbaggers! Scalawags! Just look at them taking advantage of our pain to make money for themselves! Why, if one of them comes into my shop, I'll shoo him out so fast his hat will spin right off his head!—**Southern shopkeeper**

Thank ya, suh for these clothes to wear and food for my fam'ly. We have nothin'. Don't know what we'd do without the Freedman's Bureau to help us. It seems like everyone else is ag'in us.—**freed slave***

*The Freedman's Bureau was a federal agency formed to help former slaves get food, clothing, medical care, and fair treatment after the war.

Tenants ain't got no chance. I don't know who gets the money, but it ain't the poor. It gets worse every year—the land gets more wore out, the price for tobacco gets lower, and everything you got to buy gets higher. Like I said, I'm trying to 'be content' like the Bible says and not to worry, but I don't see no hope.—**sharecropper's wife**

We have great hopes for the Fourteenth Amendment! It grants equality to all citizens, but big problems still exist between blacks and whites in the South. Southern states have passed Black Codes—laws to deny former slaves their rights. There is still such violence…will they ever embrace each other?—**Northern Congressman**

So far from engaging in a war to perpetuate slavery, I am rejoiced that slavery is abolished. I believe it will be greatly for the interest of the South. So fully am I satisfied of this that I would have cheerfully lost all that I have lost by the war and have suffered all that I have suffered to have this object obtained.—**Robert E. Lee***

*Robert E. Lee spent the rest of his life as President of Washington and Lee University in Lexington, Virginia

I cannot help but feel sad and depressed…at the downfall of a foe who fought so long and valiantly, and had suffered so much for a cause, though that cause was, I believe, one of the worst for which people ever fought.—**Ulysses S. Grant**

Today, I have been elected to the United States Senate! I'm the first black man elected to the U.S. Senate! I must work to protect the rights of my black brethren. They have a steep hill to climb.— **Hiram Revels**, Mississippi

I'll be the first black man to cast my vote after the Fifteenth Amendment grants blacks the right to vote. My parents were slaves…and here I am! What a privilege! What an honor! I can't wait to vote!—**Thomas Mundy Peterson**

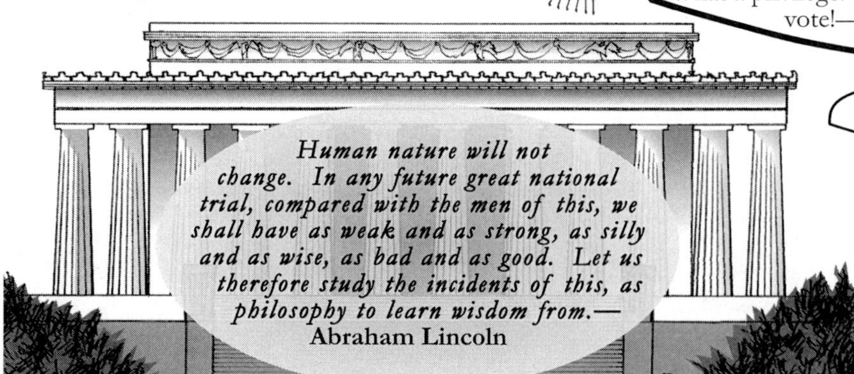

g'night John Boy
g'night Mama
g'night Tecumseh
g'night Robert E.
g'…
Lights out, boys!
g'night Stonewall

Rights Act…1868…14th Amendment to the Constitution guarantees equal rights…1870…15th Amendment grants blacks right to vote.

and Serena Williams are the first African American world doubles tennis champions…Disney unveils The Princess and the Frog, the studio's first animated film featuring an African American princess.